Penguin Specials fill a gap. Written by some of today's most exciting and insightful writers, they are short enough to be read in a single sitting — when you're stuck on a train; in your lunch hour; between dinner and bedtime. Specials can provide a thought-provoking opinion, a primer to bring you up to date, or a striking piece of fiction. They are concise, original and affordable.

To browse digital and print Penguin Specials titles, please refer to **www.penguin.com.au/penguinspecials**

City of Protest

A recent history of dissent in Hong Kong

ANTONY DAPIRAN

PENGUIN BOOKS

UK | USA | Canada | Ireland | Australia
India | New Zealand | South Africa | China

Penguin Books is part of the Penguin Random House group of companies
whose addresses can be found at global.penguinrandomhouse.com.

First published by Penguin Group (Australia), 2017

3 5 7 9 10 8 6 4 2

Cover design by Di Suo © Penguin Group (Australia)
Text design by Steffan Leyshon-Jones © Penguin Group (Australia)
Printed and bound in Hong Kong by Printing Express

penguin.com.au

ISBN: 9780734399625

CONTENTS

Preface.. 1

I   A Colony in Turmoil 11

II   The Anxious 1980s and
     Remembering Tiananmen............................... 21

III Opposing Article 23 34

IV   Heritage and Identity in the 2000s 51

V   The Umbrella Movement 69

VI   Towards 2047... 94

Notes.. 111

Photographs.. 123

Acknowledgements 125

Preface

The mid-autumn afternoon sun has sunk behind the office blocks of Hong Kong's Central business district.

I am standing in the midst of a crowd of thousands of protesters; collectively, we are blocking an eight-lane dual carriage highway. That morning, organisers had declared the beginning of the 'Occupy Central' protest campaign and called upon Hong Kongers to join student protesters in demanding political reforms. Hong Kongers had responded in their thousands, flooding the streets and facing a police cordon that prevented them from joining the student protesters outside Hong Kong government headquarters.

On the far side of the police line, students wave back at the gathering crowds. The crowd calls for police to open the road so they can join the protesters inside police lines. Inexplicably – given that opening access to the protest site would seemingly be the best way to clear the road – the police continue to hold their line.

The pressure quickly intensifies as protesters, shielded with umbrellas, raincoats and cling film, begin pushing up against the police line, and police use pepper spray to force them back. To cries of 'Ze! Ze!' ('Umbrellas!'), more umbrellas are passed through the crowd towards the front line.

Emergency access paths are opened up to enable people hit with pepper spray to make their way to the ad hoc first aid stations, marked by improvised cardboard 'First Aid' signs, where volunteers rinse out the eyes of pepper spray victims. I see a man with a bright red face, eyes streaming with tears, as he staggers up from a first aid station and heads back towards the front line. He gives me a grin and says: 'Go again!'

Behind their riot shields, I see the police slip on gas masks, I presume to protect themselves against stray bursts of pepper spray.

In the midst of this chaos, Democratic Party founder and senior statesman Martin Lee and pro-democracy media magnate Jimmy Lai come down into the midst of the crowd. They give speeches over a megaphone, calling upon people to persist but to avoid violence. Their speeches have only just ended when, without warning, there are several loud bangs and pops, and a cloud of smoke drifts over the crowd.

The realisation dawns on me slowly:

That's tear gas.

Everyone seems frozen for a moment. Time stops. Then, as the cloud of smoke drifts lazily over us, the crowd breaks. We run.

An acrid smell, like gunpowder, drifts through the air. My cheeks tingle and my eyes begin to sting. I hold my breath and make for the far side of a nearby over-pass where the air appears to be clear.

'Are you okay?' Someone in the crowd offers me water, a face mask and a wet towel.

More bangs and more clouds of gas as the police fire again.

Some people begin to throw water bottles and rub-bish at the police, but are immediately held back by the crowd: 'Don't throw anything!'

Through the rolling clouds of gas, a man emerges defiantly holding aloft two tattered umbrellas. His image is captured by press photographers and he will become the movement's icon: Umbrella Man.

But now, as the gas begins to disperse, the crowds regroup. Protesters shout at the riot police:

'Shame on you!'

'We are all Hong Kongers!'

'Take off your uniforms and go home!'

The crowd moves in towards the police again. As the gathered masses shift and surge around me, a man to my left grabs my arm and says to me urgently: 'Hong Kong is dead!'

*

Hong Kong is a city of protest. While the Umbrella Movement protests of 2014 captured the world's attention, they were merely the latest and largest iteration of an ongoing series of political protests in Hong Kong stretching back decades, including a particularly lively recent past since the return of sovereignty to China in 1997. According to Hong Kong police statistics, there were 1142 public processions in 2015, equivalent to more than three per day, in the city of 7 million people.[1]

Hong Kongers are renowned for being pragmatic, and there is indeed a pragmatic reason for protesting in Hong Kong: it often works. In many cases, protesters' demands have been met, most notably overturning the Article 23 anti-subversion legislation in 2003, forcing Chief Executive Tung Chee-Hwa's resignation following protests in 2004 and scrapping the Moral and National Education Curriculum in 2012. Over many years, Hong Kongers have been conditioned to view protest as an effective means of forcing political change in their city. According to a survey conducted by the Chinese University of Hong Kong, a quarter of Hong Kong's population agrees with the sentiment: 'Only radical action can get the government to respond to citizens' demands.'[2]

However, this pragmatic explanation is only the beginning. There are deeper cultural and structural forces driving public protest in Hong Kong. In a city whose population identifies itself – at least vis-à-vis its sovereign, the People's Republic of China – by reference to the rights and freedoms it enjoys which the rest of China's population does not, protest is an embodiment of that identity, embracing as it does the freedoms of speech, expression and assembly.

Meanwhile, Hong Kong's protests have become a tourist attraction, with the *Lonely Planet* travel guides recommending Hong Kong's protest culture to their readers when naming Hong Kong one of their top destinations, painting a picture of a pseudo Mardi Gras atmosphere: 'Rallies are infused with theatrics and eruptions of song, dance and poetry, reflecting the city's vibrant indie music and literary scenes.'[3]

But beyond the spectacle itself, the vibrancy of Hong Kong's protest culture has a greater significance. The authorities' tolerance of and reaction to public protests serve as a barometer of the health of the unique 'One Country, Two Systems' principle under which sovereignty over Hong Kong was returned to China, as well as of Beijing's disposition towards Hong Kong and its freedoms.

By extension, that reflects China's own future. Will Beijing permit the rest of China to become more open, a reflection of the Hong Kong experiment? Or will Hong Kong be forced to converge with an unyielding China as we approach 2047, the year when the fifty-year guarantee of Hong Kong's rights and freedoms expires?

The Umbrella Movement of 2014 was the crucible in which these questions were tested. Hundreds of thousands of protesters took to the streets to voice their demands for political reforms, blockading and occupying the business and commercial heart of the city for seventy-nine days. While the protesters' demands – at least for now – have gone unanswered, the movement marked a new high point for political protest in Hong Kong.

The Umbrella Movement unfolded on my doorstep. My commute from my Admiralty apartment to my office in Central was transformed from a twenty-minute trudge along heavily trafficked roads into a daily carnival. Every night I would join curious office workers stopping by on the way home from work, picking my way between rows of brightly coloured tents on the occupied highway, browsing through the latest artwork or enjoying an ad hoc musical performance. Crowds would gather to listen to student leaders standing on the makeshift speaker's platform, a plank between a couple of step ladders, addressing the crowd through a PA system powered by a diesel generator. On the side lines, a pensioner may deliver an impassioned political lecture, or a group of students engage in debate on the next steps for the movement.

The protests tore apart and remade the fabric of Hong Kong's urban landscape. The physical space itself, the highway occupied by the protesters, engendered a feeling of both transgression and liberation. In a city known for 'reclamations' of land from the ever-shrinking Victoria Harbour, this was a real reclamation. There was a sense not of taking something, but of taking something *back*; the people had reclaimed their city. A place once so unfriendly to pedestrians, so highly urbanised, so isolating and inaccessible, became – against all expectations – the most humanistic of spaces. Roads became footpaths, highways became public squares, cars and buses were banished.

Vast banners hung from footbridges splashed with black characters: 'I want genuine universal suffrage!' 'C.Y. Leung Resign!' The anonymous civic greenery of a roadside planter was replaced with a freshly planted organic vegetable garden. The protests prompted an outburst of creativity: posters covered the walls of public and commercial buildings, slogans and sketches in chalk decorated the roads and footpaths and walls, and the protest sites overflowed with paintings, sculptures and installations. Meanwhile, over in the ever-expanding

Homework Zone, students sat at improvised desks and worked late into the night, as volunteer tutors moved among them to offer help with homework.

The cliché of Hong Kong as a hectic, impersonal, high-pressured city was at a stroke undermined: here was a community full of generosity, kindness, self-lessness. For every inconvenience – a re-routed bus, a cancelled tram – there were unexpected new conveniences: free water, public artwork, first aid and mathematics tutoring.

As I sat talking to protesters at the front-line barricades late into the muggy tropical nights, or mingled with the crowds enjoying the craft market atmosphere on weekends, I reflected on the numerous protests I had witnessed during my fifteen years in the city. I recalled hundreds of thousands of Hong Kongers wearing black T-shirts and marching late into the night of 1 July 2003 to overturn a draconian anti-subversion law; Korean farmers in orange life jackets engaged in pitched battles with police in the narrow back streets of Wan Chai during anti-WTO protests in 2005; candlelight flickering on the faces of Hong Kongers young and old as they gathered in Victoria Park every year on 4 June to remember the Tiananmen demonstrations of 1989.

Looking back on Hong Kong's long and vibrant history of public protest, I realised that the Umbrella Movement was not just an isolated event but part of an ongoing narrative, a narrative intertwined with the city's very history as it transitioned from a colonial outpost to a bustling trade entrepôt to a dazzling Asian financial centre, and as it navigated its way from being the last outpost of the British Empire to reunification with a rapidly developing China. At every point along this journey, Hong Kongers have taken to the streets of their city to voice their hopes, fears and dreams.

In this book I explore the role of protest in Hong Kong life, and place the Umbrella Movement in the context of Hong Kong's history of protest. I try to understand what it is that has made political protest such an important part of the Hong Kong way-of-life. And what might the prospects be for Hong Kong's – and therefore China's – future?

As I began to investigate this history, I quickly learned that the Umbrella Movement was not the first time tear gas had been deployed against demonstrators in Hong Kong. Leafing through a book of historical photographs, I experienced a jolt of recognition when I came across an old photograph of Hong Kong police politely holding black banners reading: 'Warning: Tear Smoke'. They were the same black banners I had seen when police unleashed their tear gas canisters on that autumn afternoon in 2014. I realised that to begin to understand Hong Kong's modern protest culture, I would need to look back more than fifty years, to a decade that saw turbulent protests not just on the streets of Hong Kong but all around the world: the 1960s.

Antony Dapiran
Hong Kong
November 2016

I

A Colony in Turmoil

Hong Kong in the 1960s was a city under extreme pressure.[1] A capitalist remnant of the British Empire perched precariously on the edge of a hostile communist China, the colony strained under huge inflows of refugees from the Mainland who crowded into shanty-towns and squatter colonies. Many were without work and lived in extreme poverty. Those who could find employment often struggled in sweatshop conditions, with no protection for basic labour rights.

In 1966, the Star Ferry Company announced a proposal to increase fares by ten cents. This was at a time when the ferry was a vital public service, providing the only link between Hong Kong Island and the Kowloon peninsula. The proposal drew widespread protests from media and the community.

On 4 April 1966, a young man, So Sau-chung,

appeared at the Star Ferry concourse in Central, holding a banner with the words: 'Staging hunger strike. Opposing fare increase.' So later said that his protest had been inspired by the non-violent activism of Gandhi. He quickly attracted public support and a number of young people joined him in his hunger strike.

So was arrested the next day after refusing to leave the Star Ferry concourse, but more protesters soon gathered in Kowloon to demand his release. When police tried to arrest these protesters, the crowd grew and the protests escalated into four days of rioting, looting and arson in Mong Kok and nearby neighbourhoods. By the time it was over, 1465 people had been arrested, twenty-six were injured (including ten police officers) and one was dead.

However, the protests did accomplish their original goal: several weeks later, the government granted the Star Ferry Company a fare increase of only five cents, and only for first class tickets.

Elsie Tu (neé Elliott), a British social justice advocate and Hong Kong urban councillor who worked to help Hong Kong's socially disadvantaged, had led the campaign against the fare hike and was openly critical of the Colonial Secretary's handling of the riots. In the aftermath, Tu was hauled before a commission of enquiry and ultimately received the official blame for 'inciting' the demonstrators through her social justice campaigning, which resulted in her name becoming attached to what are now known as 'Elsie's Riots'.[2] However, the social inequalities Tu had highlighted – which were identified by the government in its own commission of inquiry – went unaddressed by the colonial administration. The underlying social tensions, in particular the lack of rights for workers, continued to fester and would escalate less than a year later.

Meanwhile, across the border, Mao Zedong's Great Proletarian Cultural Revolution was getting underway. By 1967, with the Cultural Revolution raging, much of China was in chaos, leading to a collapse in governance in neighbouring Guangdong province as well as to violent anti-colonial protests in Portuguese Macau. Anti-imperialist, anti-capitalist sentiment soon spread over the border into Hong Kong.

The immediate spark was the issue of workers' rights. Early 1967 saw a series of industrial disputes in Hong Kong that were organised or supported by pro-communist trade unions, in particular the Hong Kong Federation of Trade Unions, or FTU. In April, the Hong Kong Artificial Flower Company in Kowloon's San Po Kong district announced onerous new conditions for workers, which would reduce wages and job security. When workers protested, seeking to negotiate with management, the company responded by dismissing over 600 employees, prompting strikes and protests outside the factory gates. With support from the FTU, the dispute escalated into violent confrontations, which spread to nearby Kowloon neighbourhoods. Police and protesters clashed, and tear gas was used to disperse the crowds.

In May, loyalist groups, led and coordinated by the Hong Kong branch of the Xinhua News Agency (Beijing's *de facto* embassy in pre-1997 Hong Kong), turned the focus of their protests to the British colonial authorities themselves. Pro-Beijing protesters, brandishing copies of Chairman Mao's *Little Red Book* and shouting anti-British slogans, came together to blockade Government House. In Central, the Bank of China building was plastered with 'big character posters' denouncing the 'British imperialists', and revolutionary messages were broadcast over a loudspeaker.[3] The protests soon deteriorated into confrontations with police and further violence.

The chaos continued throughout the summer of 1967. Widespread strikes and work stoppages affected public transport and utilities through May and into June. Then, in July and August, a series of terrorist bombings rocked the city. Some reports alleged that the bombs were made in the classrooms of left-wing schools and planted indiscriminately on the city's streets. In one incident, which hardened public sentiment against the agitators and in support of the colonial administration, a seven-year-old girl and her two-year-old brother were killed by a bomb while playing outside their North Point home.

By the time the disorder was brought to an end in the September of 1967, fifty-one people had been killed (including ten police officers) and 832 injured. Police reported over 8000 suspected bombs, of which over 1000 were genuine. Almost 2000 people were convicted of various offences, including rioting, unlawful assembly and explosive offences.[4]

The 1967 riots were the worst incidence of mass violence in Hong Kong in the post-Second World War era. However, while the disturbances alarmed the local community and the British administration, and though the violence and loss of life were deplorable, the protests of 1966–1967 are credited with being the catalyst for the wide-ranging social reforms implemented in Hong Kong in the 1970s.[5] They highlighted deep social problems in Hong Kong: poverty, inequality, a lack of labour rights and inadequate education and housing. Hong Kong at the time had no social security system, no unemployment insurance and no public pension or retirement scheme. The riots drew government attention to these issues and prompted a rapid, broad-ranging response.

Maximum working hours were reduced, and new employment legislation enacted. A raft of labour reforms including improved health and safety stand-ards, workers' compensation and employment con-tract protections were introduced. Governor Murray MacLehose, after commencing his tenure in 1971, introduced additional progressive social reforms seek-ing to address inequality, including new public housing programmes, universal compulsory free education and broader government support for the provision of medi-cal and social welfare services.

The legislative response, however, was not uniformly progressive. In November 1967, Hong Kong's colonial administration sought to consolidate and toughen laws governing public assembly and 'breach of the peace'; the laws were intended to define what did and did not constitute 'acceptable' protest.

The result was the Public Order Ordinance of 1967, which required any public meeting or procession to obtain a licence from the commissioner of police. It also gave police the power to prohibit or order the dis-continuance of any public gathering if they deemed it in the interest of public order. In addition, the law granted police wide powers to arrest citizens for engag-ing in 'unlawful assembly' if police felt their behaviour could lead to a breach of the peace. The law effectively criminalised unsanctioned protests.

The ordinance was not uncontroversial at the time. In his speech presenting the law to the Legislative

Council in November 1967, Attorney General Denys Roberts acknowledged criticisms that the law went too far and was 'a backward piece of colonialism', but nevertheless argued:

> It is a problem as old as the law itself, to find the proper point of balance between citizen and state. This point, as the history of any country will show, changes from time to time. It is to be hoped that this Bill has found the right balance, taking into account, as must be done, our circumstances at the present time. If these change [...] then the Government will be ready and willing to consider suitable amendment.[6]

Notwithstanding Roberts' sentiment, that point of balance would not change for a very long time. Indeed, apart from a brief change in the mid-1990s, it would remain in place fifty years later.

Still, the protests of the 1960s can be seen as a qualified success. Faced with difficult living conditions under a colonial administration that provided no channel for political participation or expression, Hong Kongers made their opinions heard through the only means at their disposal: public protest. Notably, MacLehose subsequently introduced a system of 'district officers' to improve communication between Hong Kong citizens and the colonial government, providing a mechanism for grievances to be aired.

The Star Ferry Protest of 1966 and the leftist riots of 1967 laid the foundation for a recurring pattern of political protest in Hong Kong in the decades that followed. Time and again, the Hong Kong people, faced with a limited means of political expression, have found protest to be a successful way of achieving change. The rights and freedoms of expression and assembly that support this tradition would come to be referred to as 'Hong Kong Core Values', and were enshrined in the post-handover constitution.

The riots also increased awareness of social problems in the city and encouraged the community to become more outspoken about its dissatisfaction with the government. This would result in another series of successful protests in the early 1970s, when a scandal involving a chief superintendent of police who fled overseas to escape a corruption investigation prompted community outrage and student-led protests. The MacLehose administration responded by appointing a judicial inquiry whose recommendations led to the establishment of Hong Kong's Independent Commission Against Corruption, a landmark in the city's legal and social history.

In order to win public support for their actions to quell the 1967 unrest, the colonial government appealed to a sense of community and citizenship among the local populace, encouraging people to think of Hong Kong as home, and citing the need to maintain stability and prosperity. For a population that included many people who had fled to Hong Kong seeking refuge from hardships in the Mainland – whether during the Sino-Japanese and civil wars of the 1930s and '40s, Mao's disastrous Great Leap Forward in the 1950s or the Cultural Revolution in the 1960s – the appeal resonated and took hold. It is perhaps ironic that today's pro-Beijing advocates in Hong Kong, in their attempt to win the support of the populace, adopt the same discourse of 'prosperity and stability' that was once directed against them by the colonial authorities.

However, the events of 1967 also revealed the impact that a hostile China could have on Hong Kong. This convinced the British government that a negotiated return of Hong Kong to Beijing's rule was the only realistic future for its colony. A 1968 report by the Defence and Overseas Policy Committee concluded: 'There is no real prospect of any solution which does not provide for the resumption of Chinese sovereignty over Hong Kong.'[7]

In Beijing, Premier Zhou Enlai was said to view the 1967 riots as one of the many excesses of the Cultural Revolution. Seeking to dampen the enthusiasm of leftist agitators in Hong Kong, Zhou reportedly said: 'We do not intend to take back Hong Kong immediately, nor do we plan to wage a war against Britain . . . It doesn't work if we copy the practices of the Red Guards to Hong Kong.'[8] Beijing settled on a policy towards Hong Kong that saw the issue as a 'legacy from the past . . . that, when conditions are ripe . . . should be settled peacefully through negotiations and that, pending a settlement, the status quo should be maintained.'[9]

In this way, the protests set the course for the very future of Hong Kong.

II

The Anxious 1980s and
Remembering Tiananmen

On the last day of negotiations before the signing of
the Sino-British Joint Declaration on Hong Kong in
1984, Sir David Wilson, lead negotiator for the British
side and future governor of Hong Kong, emerged from
the negotiation room pumping his fist in triumph. He
announced to his fellow members of the British delegation: 'We got elections!'[1]

Wilson was referring to the process for selecting
Hong Kong's Legislative Council, LegCo, after the
handover. The Chinese had held out until the final
hour before conceding that LegCo would be constituted by way of elections. In exchange, the British settled for the chief executive (the post-handover
equivalent of governor of the territory) to be appointed
by Beijing on the basis of 'elections or consultations'
to be held in Hong Kong.[2] This in itself was a higher

standard than that which applied to Britain's governor, who was appointed by Whitehall without any consultations, let alone elections, in Hong Kong.

The outcome of the negotiations was reflected in Hong Kong's constitution, the Basic Law, which states that the 'ultimate aim' is for the chief executive to be selected by 'universal suffrage'.[3] The question for Hong Kongers with democratic aspirations therefore became: When and how would this 'ultimate aim' be realised?

However, in 1989 anxieties over future electoral mechanics paled in significance to far more urgent events in China. As student protests spread across the Mainland that spring, Hong Kongers donated funds and goods to support the protesters. As Sir Percy Craddock, British Foreign Office mandarin and Margaret Thatcher's key advisor on Hong Kong, subsequently recounted: 'I recall that Jiang Zemin took me to the window of the Great Hall of the People, pointed out to the Square and said, there were the tents and they were put up with Hong Kong money.'[4]

The day after martial law was imposed in Beijing on Saturday, 21 May 1989, over 600 000 Hong Kongers marched to express their solidarity with the students in Tiananmen Square, and to demand the resignation of hard-line Chinese Premier Li Peng. At the rally, democratic scion Szeto Wah inaugurated a new coalition of pro-democratic political groups, the Hong Kong

Alliance in Support of the Patriotic Democratic Movement in China. The rally was notable for the support it attracted not only from pro-democratic figures, but also from prominent figures of the entertainment and business worlds, as well as traditionally left-wing groups such as the FTU and pro-Beijing media like the *Ta Kung Pao* newspaper. Even local employees of the Xinhua News Agency reportedly participated.[5]

On Sunday, 28 May, with rumours that a military crackdown to clear Tiananmen Square was imminent, an even larger crowd of 1.5 million people took to the streets. It was the largest protest in Hong Kong's history, and part of a worldwide day of protest. The march, which lasted more than eight hours, began in Central and wound its way along the length of Hong Kong Island. As the first group of marchers reached the end of the fifteen-kilometre route, others were still waiting to begin. Parents carried children on their shoulders; others pushed the elderly in wheelchairs. A yacht sailed through the harbour with pro-democracy slogans painted on its sails. Students from the Academy of Performing Arts performed songs to entertain the crowd, including a pop anthem specially composed by local Canto-pop stars to support the students. In a telling statement of Hong Kongers' anxiety about their own future post-1997, many held signs reading: 'Today China, Tomorrow Hong Kong'.[6]

Hong Kong has hosted vigils to commemorate 4 June annually since 1989. Organised by the Alliance, the Tiananmen vigils originally focused on supporting democracy in China. The Alliance included as part of its policy platform the release of all dissidents, a reassessment of the official account of the 1989 protests, the end of one-party rule and the establishment of a democratic China. However, while concern for the Mainland was genuine, the protests also were underlain with apprehension about Hong Kong. Many had criticised the 1984 Joint Declaration for failing to give Hong Kongers enough of a say in their own future. After 1989, it was commonly said that Britain had 'sold Hong Kong down the river'.[7] Protesting in support of the students in Beijing was perhaps the best way for Hong Kongers to express their frustration at the Joint Declaration that had decided their fate without their direct input.

The unprecedented scale of the protests in 1989 demonstrated to the British colonial administration the widespread anger and pessimism among Hong Kongers faced with an uncertain future under Beijing's rule. In response, Hong Kong's LegCo passed the Hong Kong Bill of Rights Ordinance. Aimed at reassuring both Hong Kong residents and – perhaps more importantly to both the British and Chinese governments – international investors in the territory, the

Bill of Rights incorporated the key provisions of the International Covenant on Civil and Political Rights into Hong Kong's domestic law. Rights protected by the bill included freedom of opinion, expression and association, as well as the right of peaceful assembly.[8]

The last governor of Hong Kong, Chris Patten, who assumed office in July 1992, five years before the handover, championed these rights and pushed reforms even further. Patten argued that the success of post-handover Hong Kong depended upon it remaining an open and plural society. Patten declared midway through his term:

> We have to complete the work we have set in hand to preserve and enhance civil liberties in Hong Kong, so the community gets what the Bill of Rights promises. We will complete the work of securing press freedom on the statute book, of enhancing the rights of women and the disabled, of making government more open and accountable, and of giving the citizen easier redress for grievances.[9]

With his last point, Patten perhaps sought to improve the imperfect system with which Hong Kong found itself, by giving citizens an effective alternative to protests when it came to airing grievances.

The importance of these rights and freedoms began to coalesce in Hong Kong around the development of a unique identity, which came to be referred to – in official government discourse, in the media and around tea house tables in Hong Kong – as 'Hong Kong Core Values'. The term came to be used to encapsulate those freedoms and safeguards that distinguished the Hong Kong way of life for many of its citizens. Hong Kong Core Values included: one of the world's freest economies, a lively and unfettered media, the right to participate (to varying degrees) in the electoral and governing process, freedom to criticise the government, unrestricted travel, rule of law and due process, an independent judiciary, accountability and clean government and, of course, the right to protest.

Hong Kong Core Values were also defined by what they were not. Especially in the wake of 1989, they were emphatically not Communism or 'Mainland values'. Hong Kongers looked across the border and saw a nation plagued by corruption, where unarmed student and civilian protesters had been crushed by the army; where dissidents had been summarily rounded up and jailed for protesting and speaking out against the government; and where all information about these events had been suppressed. Hong Kong was proudly a key terminus in the 'underground railway' charged with spiriting out of China those dissidents who needed to escape Beijing's dragnet. Hong Kong's rights and freedoms – just as much as the right to conduct business and make money under a capitalist system – were what Hong Kongers felt distinguished their lives from the rest of the country to which they would soon be returned.

In order to provide some assurance to the Hong Kong people that these Core Values would be protected by law after the handover, Britain had negotiated to ensure that they were included in the Joint Declaration:

> Rights and freedoms, including those of the person, of speech, of the press, of assembly, of association, of travel, of movement, of correspondence, of strike, of choice of occupation, of academic research and of religious belief will be ensured by law in the Hong Kong Special Administrative Region.[10]

However, while the text was agreed upon by Britain and China, the interpretation would be subject to ongoing disputes. The disparity between what Governor Patten and Beijing viewed as the rights and freedoms Hong Kong should enjoy was made clear in the dispute over what should constitute 'acceptable protest' under the Public Order Ordinance.

In 1995, Patten ordered that the Public Order Ordinance – still largely unchanged from when it was enacted following the 1967 riots – be amended to relax restrictions on citizens' political freedoms, and that it be brought into line with the provisions of the International Covenant on Civil and Political Rights. Protesters would simply need to *notify* the commissioner of police rather than seek permission. In addition, police powers to summarily prohibit or discontinue public gatherings would be curtailed.

However, the Beijing leadership was furious at Patten's democratic reforms, which it saw as an attempt to unilaterally renegotiate the Joint Declaration and 'sabotage' Hong Kong prior to the handover. In February 1997, China's National People's Congress announced that Patten's reforms would not be adopted post-1997.[11] The legislature elected under Patten's electoral reforms was dismissed, and the Provisional Legislative Council – a transitional Hong Kong legislature appointed by Beijing – introduced a series of legislation rolling back Patten's initiatives. Included in this revision was an amended Public Order Ordinance, which effectively reintroduced the colonial licensing system for public gatherings and also permitted police to prohibit a public procession in the interests of 'national security'.[12]

Even today, the Public Order Ordinance exists in similar terms to those enacted in 1967. Under the law as it currently stands, any gathering or procession of fifty people or more which has not obtained prior consent of the commissioner of police risks being declared an 'unauthorised assembly'. Organising or participating in an unauthorised assembly is a criminal offence, subject to penalties of up to five years' jail time.[13]

This is the very law that protest organisers referred to during the first days of the Umbrella Movement protests of 2014, when they announced ominously over loudspeakers:

> Police have refused to extend our permission for this protest. As of midnight this will become an unauthorised assembly and you will be at risk of arrest. If you wish to leave, please do so now.

Many Umbrella Movement protesters were arrested and charged under the Public Order Ordinance. It is remarkable that a piece of colonial-era legislation – criticised at the time of its introduction almost fifty years ago as excessive and unjustified – should still be used to police political expression in the twenty-first century.

Today, Hong Kong government officials constantly point to Hong Kong's Core Values as being a defining characteristic of the city. Indeed, Chief Executive C.Y. Leung himself reiterated this in his 2015 policy speech: 'The Government remains committed to upholding core values such as freedom, human rights, democracy, the rule of law and clean governance.'[14]

These Core Values lie at the heart of Hong Kong's identity, particularly as distinguished from the rest of

China. At one time in history, this distinction might have been made on the basis of wealth: Hong Kong was rich, while China was struggling to bring its population out of poverty. Many in Hong Kong thought of their Mainland cousins as poor, unsophisticated bumpkins, a far cry from the urban sophisticates living in the bright lights of Hong Kong. However, as Hong Kong's economy languished and China's boomed in the first decade of the twenty-first century, that distinction has failed to hold and Hong Kongers found themselves reliant on those same Mainland cousins to support Hong Kong's tourism- and service-based economy.

With this pride rooted in materialism tidily undermined, there emerged a deeper pride among Hong Kongers, based on the rule of law, civil liberties, rights and freedoms and clean and accountable government.[15] 'Hong Kong Core Values' became the answer to the question: 'What does it mean to be a Hong Kong citizen?' In circumstances where the government was not in a position to offer electoral rights or participatory democracy, the official emphasis on civil liberties and freedoms became a source of both identity and legitimacy for successive regimes.

Hong Kong Core Values are on display every year at the Tiananmen vigil held in Hong Kong. The vigil held on 4 June 1998 marked the first time that the Tiananmen incident had been publicly commemorated on Chinese sovereign soil. However, the Hong Kong government clearly remains ambivalent about Hong Kong's special status in this regard. Leading Tiananmen-era dissidents, including Wang Dan, one of the key student leaders in 1989, have been consistently refused visas to enter Hong Kong after the handover.

Exiting the Causeway Bay subway station to attend a 4 June vigil, you emerge onto a neon-lit shopping strip. On this night, unlike other nights, the street will be crammed not with shoppers but with politicians and activists, promoting their causes and soliciting donations from the crowds as people make their way towards Victoria Park. Police shepherd the crowds towards the floodlit sports pitches at the southern side of the park, where the mood grows increasingly more sombre.

The park fills as tens of thousands of demonstrators of all ages file in, their faces illuminated by flickering candles. The park, ringed with apartment and office towers, is a forest of candlelight. At its centre stand replicas of the Goddess of Democracy, the statue made famous during the Tiananmen protests, and the Monument to the People's Heroes, the column standing at the centre of Tiananmen Square where the students made their last stand. These are surrounded by funeral wreaths.

The vigil is presided over by democratic politicians representing the Alliance. They give speeches and lead the crowd in singing patriotic songs from the

Protesters hold their candles aloft at the Tiananmen Vigil in Victoria Park, June 2015

Tiananmen era; current activists fighting for human rights on the Mainland give video addresses on large screens.

Participation numbers at the 4 June vigil in the years after 1989 seemed to reflect events in Hong Kong more than the Mainland. In the immediate post-handover years, as life continued as normal in Hong Kong, attendance at the annual vigils dwindled to just tens of thousands. It was only in 2009, twelve years after the handover and twenty years after Tiananmen, that attendance returned to over 100 000 each year. In that year, then-Chief Executive Donald Tsang said he was representing the opinion of the majority of Hong Kongers when he stated that 4 June was something that 'happened many years ago', and that Hong Kong people should 'make an objective assessment of the nation's development'. Many Hong Kongers joined the vigil to emphasise that, unlike Tsang, they did not consider Tiananmen to be 'history'.[16]

It is no coincidence that increased enthusiasm for commemorating the 4 June protests in the years leading up to the 2014 Umbrella Movement demonstrations should coincide with increased dissatisfaction with governance in Hong Kong, and with the implementation of the 'One Country, Two Systems' model. Whereas the protests were once intended to express support for the freedom of fellow Chinese citizens across the border, the annual vigils have more recently become an outlet to express anxiety about Hong Kong's future. A significant reason for that anxiety is that the city's Core Values are under threat of being supplanted by Mainland values. By remembering 4 June, Hong Kongers remind themselves and their government what those competing Mainland values represent, and why Hong Kong's Core Values are worth fighting to maintain. They are, after all, the only thing that enables such protests to continue in Hong Kong at all.

III

Opposing Article 23

As the 1990s wore on and 1 July 1997 approached, anxiety in Hong Kong began to ease and many faced the handover with equanimity if not optimism. Beijing and London managed to negotiate resolutions to many contentious issues ahead of the handover, while the ghosts of Tiananmen began to fade and the Beijing leadership was gradually rehabilitated on the world stage. Deng Xiaoping engineered a resurgence of economic growth on the Mainland after his famous Southern Tour of 1992, and people in Hong Kong put their apprehensions behind them as property prices boomed and the stock market surged, with investors particularly clamouring for stocks in 'red chip' Mainland companies.

In the end, however, any post-handover glow in Hong Kong was short-lived and the years immediately following were economically and politically challenging.

The Asian Financial Crisis of 1997–1998 began on the day after the handover, when the Thai government announced that it would float the *baht*. Speculative attacks on the Hong Kong dollar's peg to the US dollar followed, the Hang Seng Index dropped 23 per cent over three days in October 1997 and property prices crashed. Many property investors suddenly found themselves in a position of 'negative equity', their properties worth less than the amounts owed on their mortgages. Regional economies began to stabilise by 1999, only to suffer again from market disruptions following 11 September 2001. Finally, from November 2002 through mid-2003, Hong Kong found itself at the epicentre of a global health epidemic when Severe Acute Respiratory Syndrome (SARS) killed 299 people in Hong Kong. The ensuing panic devastated the local economy, with tourism being particularly hard hit.

The administration of Tung Chee-Hwa, the Hong Kong Special Administrative Region's first chief executive, was ill-equipped to deal with the challenges of these turbulent years. The affable Tung proved an ineffectual administrator with a tin ear for politics. He introduced an affordable housing plan, only to withdraw it after it contributed to the collapse in the property market; his cabinet members were accused of incompetence and dishonesty; unemployment rose to a historical high of 8.3 per cent.[1] As an ailing economy led to lay-offs and pay cuts, some union leaders reminded Tung of the painful lessons of the 1967 riots in the hope that he would take action to improve the situation.[2] It was a warning that Tung failed to heed.

By 2003, six years after the handover, popular discontent in Hong Kong had reached a boiling point. With no formalised avenues for citizens to voice their opinions and vote Tung's government out of office, Hong Kongers took to the streets.

The 2003 protests proved to be a watershed moment in Hong Kong protest history. After 2003, the number of reported 'public order events' in Hong Kong would increase dramatically, from 1975 events in 2004 to 6029 events in 2015.[3] The years following 2003 also saw increased activism from Hong Kong civil society groups seeking to participate in the policy-making process, particularly in the heritage and environmental areas.

From all appearances, the 2003 protests seem to mark the moment at which Hong Kongers realised that public protest is perhaps the only effective means of political expression available in post-handover Hong Kong. To understand why this is the case, it is necessary to understand Hong Kong's system of governance, which has aptly been described as 'the result of collusion between Hong Kong's tycoons and Beijing's Communists'.[4]

The chief executive wields significant power in

Hong Kong, making key appointments throughout the Hong Kong government. From the ministers or secretaries responsible for key portfolios and government departments to the officials and board members of bodies as diverse as the Independent Commission Against Corruption, the Securities and Futures Commission and Hong Kong's public universities, a wide variety of positions are filled according to the chief executive's decisions. Also responsible for setting government policy, the chief executive and relevant ministers formulate the budget and introduce legislation into the legislature.

Under the current method for selecting Hong Kong's chief executive, put in place in 2012, candidates are elected by an election committee of 1200 representatives drawn from various industry, business, social and government groups.[5] Given that the majority of these representatives are selected by the pro-Beijing business community, the resulting committee is composed predominantly of pro-Beijing loyalists. A minimum of 150 votes from the election committee are required to nominate a candidate, and the election committee then conducts successive rounds of voting until one of the candidates wins a clear majority and is declared the winner. As a result, the most powerful figure in Hong Kong, the chief executive, does not enjoy any popular mandate from the broader citizenry.

Hong Kong's legislature, the Legislative Council or LegCo, is nominally the body that enacts Hong Kong's laws. However, the power of LegCo to function as a democratically representative governing body is severely circumscribed, both through its composition and through the powers it is able to exercise.

Seventy members constitute LegCo, of which:

– Thirty-five are returned by way of 'geographic constituencies' elected by means of universal suffrage. These seats are similar to parliamentary seats in the lower house of Westminster systems such as that in the United Kingdom or Australia, or to congressional districts in the United States. There were approximately 3.8 million registered voters for geographic constituencies in Hong Kong in 2016.[6]

– Thirty are returned by 'functional constituencies'. These are seats representing various industries, professions or other special interest groups. These include, for example, seats representing particular industries such as the textiles, transport, real estate and insurance industries, seats representing professions such as the medical, legal and accounting professions and seats representing certain 'clan' groups. Only members of the particular group are permitted to vote for their representative. Thus, for instance, only Hong Kong registered accountants may be nominated or vote for the representative in the accounting profession functional constituency. There were in total only 240 000 registered electors (which may be companies as well as individuals) across all functional constituencies in 2016.[7]

– Five are returned by the 'district council' functional constituency. These seats, introduced as a compromise between pan-democrat politicians and Beijing during electoral reforms in 2010, may only be filled by existing district councillors (members of local councils). All registered voters who are not already voting in another functional constituency may cast votes for these seats.

The result of this system in the most recent LegCo election held in September 2016 was that pro-Beijing parties won forty out of the seventy seats, with pan-democrats (a loose affiliation of broadly pro-democratic – and by implication anti-Beijing – political parties) and non-affiliated independents holding the remaining thirty seats.[8] However, these results mask the underlying inequality of the system; the pan-democrat politicians won a majority of the geographic constituency seats,[9] which are the only seats elected by universal suffrage. However, the influence of the pro-Beijing lobby among the businesses comprising the functional constituencies enabled them to win almost all of those seats,[10] ensuring that they retained majority control of the legislature. This result did not reflect the fact that the pan-democrat parties received approximately 60 per cent of the total popular vote.[11]

Authority in the Hong Kong system therefore springs from three separate power bases: the general electorate (for geographical constituencies); corporate, professional and special interest groups (for the functional constituencies); and the Beijing-friendly election committee for the chief executive. This results in fragmented authority for all branches of government, and prevents any one group from imposing its will on the other.[12] The chief executive, lacking a popular electoral mandate, is not in a position to dictate any agenda to LegCo. Nor does LegCo have the power to direct the policy programme of the chief executive and the chief executive's administration.

In terms of its powers, LegCo enacts laws like any other legislature. However, its power is circumscribed in one very important way: legislation can generally only be introduced into LegCo by the chief executive and his administration. This means that the chief executive effectively controls the legislative agenda. Private members' bills – introduced by individual members of LegCo – are permitted, but require the written consent of the chief executive (an effective veto) if they are 'relating to government policies'.[13] Of course, it is hard to envisage any kind of meaningful legislation that could *not* be argued to 'relate to government policies'. In addition, private members' bills must obtain a super majority of separate majorities of each of the geographic constituency seats and functional constituency seats, giving the pro-Beijing parties veto power over any such bills through their permanent majority of the functional constituencies.[14]

All the same, legislation does require a positive vote of a majority of LegCo to pass even government-initiated bills. Thus, the chief executive must secure the support of LegCo in order to implement his or her policies. Legislators have the power to question government officials and require them to justify their policies, their electoral mandate giving legislators a certain influence in terms of voicing the demands of the people.[15]

Finally, unlike legislatures in many other systems, LegCo does not form or produce government; ministers are not drawn from the legislature (as they are in a Westminster parliamentary system), nor does the legislature vote on ministerial appointments made by the chief executive (as in the United States, where many presidential appointments are subject to the 'advice and consent' of the Senate). Essentially, as a result of the electoral system, Hong Kongers elect the opposition, they do not elect the government.

Because of their status as the perennial opposition, the only constructive role the pan-democrat parties have to play in the policy-making process is to act as a check and balance on the executive. In fact, when it comes to their role as politicians, their participation in protest activities is just as important and arguably as effective as their actions in the legislature. Pan-democrat politicians can be seen taking the lead at protest marches, leading chants and rallying the crowds. During the Umbrella Movement, 'Long Hair' Leung Kwok-hung of the League of Social Democrats was at the front line of the blockade of the chief executive's office, coordinating protesters with a megaphone. Lawyer and former pan-democrat legislator Margaret Ng led the 'Mobile Democracy Classroom', a series of outdoor lectures on democracy and human rights. Fernando Cheung of the Labour Party and Claudia Mo of the Civic Party positioned themselves at the front of the barricades in Mong Kok, forming a human shield between police and protesters to prevent violent clashes.

Some of the pan-democrats even combine their political and protest roles in the LegCo chamber itself, with legislators from the more extreme League of Social Democrats and People's Power parties frequently engaging in protest actions from their seats during LegCo sessions, unfurling banners, chanting slogans and invariably being ejected from the chamber as a result. League of Social

Democrats legislator Raymond 'Mad Dog' Wong threw a bunch of bananas at former Chief Executive Donald Tsang during his policy speech, and more recently threw a glass of water at C.Y. Leung in a fit of pique during a LegCo question-and-answer session. His colleague, 'Long Hair' Leung, threw bitter melon and jasmine flowers at Financial Secretary John Tsang during his budget speech in protest of the budget's failure to address the 'bitter' circumstances of the working class.

*

It was this flawed post-handover political system that, in 2003, was unable to accommodate or alleviate popular discontent with Tung Chee-Hwa's administration. However, the spark that caused the ultimate conflagration was the proposed enactment of draconian new anti-subversion laws in Hong Kong. Article 23 of the Basic Law requires Hong Kong to enact legislation to 'prohibit any act of treason, secession, sedition or subversion against the Central People's Government'.[16] Six years after the handover, the legislation had still not been enacted, and in 2003 Tung's Secretary for Security, Regina Ip, proposed to enact the legislation in heavy-handed terms that would significantly curtail freedoms in Hong Kong.

On 1 July, the public holiday that commemorates the handover, the front page of the anti-establishment *Apple*

Daily newspaper screamed in huge red characters: 'Take to the streets! See you there!'[17] Over 500 000 people answered the call, marching to oppose the Article 23 anti-subversion legislation and protest Tung's administration.[18]

The Hong Kong Observatory issued a 'hot weather warning' that day; temperatures had climbed to thirty-two degrees by early afternoon when the march was due to commence. As protesters converged on Victoria Park, the subway operator MTR Corporation was forced to dispatch extra trains to cope with the large crowds. They gathered under the hot sun, dressed in black in symbolic mourning for Hong Kong, carrying banners stating 'Oppose Article 23' and 'Resign Tung Chee-Hwa'. Some carried effigies of Tung and Ip. Participants were young and old, from all walks of life. Parents carried young children on their shoulders. Prominent entertainers and media figures joined the march, as did groups representing various industries and professional bodies.

The mood of the crowd encompassed both jubilation and anger – anger at the government and the unpopular Ip, who had suggested that people would attend the rally simply because they had nothing better to do on a public holiday. Some chanted: 'We march for freedom, not for fun' in riposte.[19] But the crowd was also buoyed by the positive sense that people were united;

there was, above all, an overwhelmingly optimistic spirit.

The march wound its way through the busiest districts of Hong Kong, from Victoria Park through the Causeway Bay shopping district to Wan Chai and the government offices in Central. The crowd's voices echoed down the canyons of office and apartment towers lining the narrow streets as they shouted: 'Tung Chee-Hwa resign!' Many waited hours for their turn to march. The crowd was so large that people were still arriving at Victoria Park to begin their march hours after the first protesters arrived in Central, and the last marchers did not arrive at their final destination until nine o'clock that night, more than six hours after the march began.

It is notable that the Article 23 legislation specifically – and not merely tough economic times or an unpopular government – prompted the march. The legislation was seen as an attack on Hong Kong Core Values, provoking a strong and visceral reaction from the Hong Kong populace. They were protesting not just against an unpopular piece of legislation or a proposed curtailment of freedoms; they were protesting a threat to their very identity as Hong Kongers. And the right to protest was a fundamental part of that identity, as articulated in a commentary in the *Ming Pao* newspaper: 'Safeguarding the rights to demonstration, assembly and protest is an important foundation of Hong Kong's democratic development and building of civil society. So long as the "national security bill" is not amended, we will fight to the end!'[20]

The protest was successful. In its aftermath, Ip resigned and the legislation was withdrawn.

However, Tung continued to be unpopular, making an increasing number of policy missteps and presiding over a still-faltering economy. As a result, the 1 July holiday in 2004 again saw a significant turnout of protesters demanding Tung's resignation.[21] He finally resigned the following March, citing personal reasons, two years before his term was due to end.

Protesters at the annual 1 July march highlighting political interference in academic freedom, July 2014

Large-scale protests have been held on 1 July every year since. It must surely rankle with Beijing that the anniversary of the handover has become an annual opportunity to vent dissatisfaction with the government and voice demands for increased democracy, civil liberties and other political causes. While the essence of the annual protest remains its pro-democracy, anti-Hong Kong government message, the ambit has widened to embrace all manners of political and social causes. A typical 1 July protest hosts streetstalls promoting press freedom, academic freedom, religious freedom, women's rights, LGBTQ rights, seniors' rights, housing equality, various environmental causes (from recycling to anti-nuclear power) and the rights of animals from the Lantau Island wild oxen to sharks who die to have their fins put on Hong Kong's wedding banquet tables.

Hong Kongers recognise that, given the current method for electing a chief executive, the election of any candidate to the role – or even the successful completion of an incumbent's term – depends entirely on Beijing's perception of the chief executive's performance. The experience with Tung reinforced that. And the best way for Hong Kongers to get Beijing's attention and convey their anger to the Chinese leadership is through large and noisy public protest.

The 1 July protests caused Beijing authorities to take

a much more active and interventionist interest in Hong Kong. Under the assumption that an improved economy would reduce Hong Kongers' discontent, the Closer Economic Partnership Agreement was entered into by the Hong Kong and Mainland governments in 2003, encouraging cross-border business and investment and providing a range of incentives to Hong Kong businesses. The 'individual visit scheme', permitting Mainland tourists to visit Hong Kong without having to join a group tour, was also introduced to support Hong Kong's tourism industry, which had been severely damaged by the SARS outbreak.[22]

All in all, the 1 July 2003 protests marked a major shift in Hong Kong protest culture. They demonstrated the potential role citizens could play in the policy-making process, prompting the government to increase its use of advisory bodies and public consultations to encourage public participation in policy initiatives. Funding was increased for district councils, and their powers expanded, pushing responsibility for community-level issues down to these bodies that were closer and more responsive to the communities they served.[23]

*

While the 2003 protests helped to embolden Hong Kong's civil society groups, it was an unexpected source that provided these groups with inspiration for more extreme protest tactics. In December 2005, the World Trade Organization Ministerial Conference was hosted in Hong Kong, attracting large numbers of anti-globalisation protesters from around the region and the globe, including many Korean farmers who travelled to Hong Kong to protest against the WTO, which they saw as a threat to their livelihood. The Koreans and other international pro-testers adopted varied and colourful tactics, and were not afraid of direct confrontation with police. Hong Kong artist and activist Birdy Chu explained:

> The Anti-WTO rally in 2005 was a turning point for Hong Kong protest culture. Before then, protest was nothing but chanting slogans, holding banners, burning props, doing street dramas and handing in petitions. However in 2005, a group of young people concerned with social issues witnessed the protest methods of Korean farmers and protesters from all over the world in this international protest. It opened our minds to the concept of protest.[24]

Inspired by the WTO protests, Hong Kong citizens began consciously integrating art and spectacle into their protests as a way of capturing public and media attention.[25] They also became more willing to engage in direct confrontation with the police, a trend that would be noticeable in the heritage-focused protests of subsequent years as well as the Umbrella Movement.

Meanwhile, the crowds attending the 1 July protests began to dwindle in the years following Tung's resignation. It would take another peak of popular discontent, during the ongoing debate around democratic reforms in 2014, to spur the highest attendance since 2004. In that year, however, the 1 July protest would serve not as the highlight of Hong Kong's annual protest calendar, but as a warm-up for what was to come.

IV

Heritage and Identity in the 2000s

In the wake of the 2003 protests, the growing engagement of Hong Kong's citizens and civil society groups prompted a wave of social movements. These movements gained traction especially among the middle class, and focused on post-materialist values such as culture, heritage, social inequality and the environment.[1]

The 'borrowed time, borrowed space' attitude of the pre-1997 colonial era began to give way to a sense of local identity; Hong Kongers began to feel that this was 'our time, our space'.[2] Heritage – both tangible, in the sense of landmarks and public space, and intangible, in the sense of community and Hong Kong identity – became the new front line in a contested vision for the city's future, challenging the legitimacy of a political system that always appeared to favour the interests of property developers and the business community over the rest of its citizenry. In the words of commentator Anthony Cheung, writing at the time:

> The growing public opposition to the demolition
> of landmarks in our collective memory points
> to the rise of a new politics of identity. We are
> seeing not merely a conflict between development
> and conservation, but calls for policymakers to
> be more assertive in preserving symbols of local
> roots. Many Hong Kong Chinese are worried
> about losing the city's Hongkongness.[3]

At the same time, this heritage, both tangible and intangible, represented a reassuring link to the past at a time when Hong Kongers felt they were being threatened by an encroachment of new, Mainland values which appeared to be increasingly influencing Hong Kong government policies.

Activists recognised the limited role of the pan-democrats in LegCo. Thus, with little prospect of effecting change within the institutional arena, activists turned once again to protest, contesting individual issues directly.[4] Due to their exclusion from the formal policy-making process, these activists sought the support of public opinion and to engage in direct dialogue with the government. Coupled with protest, Hong Kong's free media and the presence of at least some independent voices in the legislature put these issues on the public agenda.

A number of protests typified these new causes: the campaigns to save the Star Ferry and Queen's Piers in Central as well as Wedding Card Street in Wan Chai, protests against a proposed high-speed rail link project cutting a swathe through rural Hong Kong, and the campaign against a Mainland-biased civics curriculum that was proposed for Hong Kong's schools.

*

The Star Ferry Pier in Central was a gem of mid-century modern architecture. The sleek, white building with its horizontal moulding and multi-paned rectangular windows was crowned by a central, Bauhaus-style clock tower. This unassuming piece of art deco was a charming counterfoil to the forest of post-modern gleaming steel and glass office towers in which it sat.

Perhaps more importantly, many saw the Star Ferry Pier as a key piece of Hong Kong's collective memory. It had been the beginning and endpoint of countless journeys between Central and Tsim Sha Tsui; some commuters had passed beneath its clock tower thousands of times. It also held particular significance as the site where So Sau-chung commenced his hunger strike, which eventually prompted the Star Ferry Riots of 1966.

As such, the pier was the 'symbolic birthplace of modern social activism' in Hong Kong.[5]

Meanwhile, the adjacent Queen's Pier garnered its own fair share of nostalgia as the place of disembarkation for visiting royals, including the Queen in 1975 and Prince Charles and Princess Diana in 1989. Cultural heritage and the collective memory associated with these locations were also embodied in Hong Kong cinema, as one protester explained in reference to Queen's Pier: 'You can say this is a symbol of the colonial period but it's much more than this . . . if we look at our local films, a lot of scenes are taken here. It really belongs to Hong Kong people.'[6]

In 1999, an ambitious new harbour reclamation and roadworks plan for Central district was unveiled. The plan would create acres of new harbour-front land, new underground railway connections and a highway bypass that would significantly reduce traffic congestion along the crowded north side of Hong Kong Island. However, it would require the demolition and relocation of the Star Ferry and Queen's Piers. The government claimed that the project was necessary for transport management purposes, and pre-emptively proposed (to head off public opposition, one can guess) that the reclaimed land be used for a world-class waterfront promenade rather than property development.

As the 2006 date for demolition drew closer, public

outcry increased. Observers noted that the government appeared to be conveniently hastening to demolish the Star Ferry Pier, which, having been built in 1957, was forty-nine years old. If it reached fifty, it would qualify to be considered for heritage protection.

Protesters began to camp out at the Star Ferry Pier days before the demolition was due to take place, staging sit-ins and artistic performances. One notable performance involved a black-clad young woman sitting atop a ladder in the street facing the clock tower, cutting off chunks of her own hair with scissors and casting them into the wind.[7] To many Hong Kongers, losing the Star Ferry Pier was like losing a piece of themselves. Even after the ceremonial final Star Ferry voyage had departed and the pier had been closed to the public, protesters still continued to break in and occupy the site. Hoardings were plastered with posters, photographs, notes and other tributes. Some students undertook a forty-nine-hour-long hunger strike, one hour for each year of the pier's existence. In a direct link back to the 1966 Star Ferry Riots, veteran protester So Sau-chung even attended to lend his support.

On the day government contractors were slated to begin their work, protesters formed a human chain in an attempt to block access. Police were called in and the protests soon became violent. Scuffles broke out as police dragged protesters away by force, resulting in several injuries. The Star Ferry Pier and its iconic clock tower were finally demolished unceremoniously in the dead of night, and the pieces sent to a landfill.

However, the protesters had succeeded in attracting the authorities' attention. As focus shifted in early January 2007 to the demolition of adjacent Queen's Pier, the secretary of the Home Affairs Department issued a statement, confirming that the protests had prompted the government to rethink its plans:

> The Government has noted citizens' recent enthusiastic attention and debate of the preservation of cultural relics, especially their feelings towards collective memory . . . As a result, the Chief Executive has instructed the Home Affairs Department to undertake further public consultation in relation to the policy on protection of heritage buildings.[8]

By the end of March, the government confirmed that it would relocate and reconstruct Queen's Pier in order to preserve the monument. When Queen's Pier was eventually dismantled in mid-2007 (amid further protests), the process was carefully documented and the pieces placed in a government storage depot. By mid-2016, the government was undertaking a public consultation process with a view to reassembling the pier on the site of the new Central Ferry Piers.[9]

*

While recognising the public concern about collective memory as it relates to heritage landmark preservation, the government nonetheless criticised the concept of collective memory as 'abstract and changeable'. Unfortunately for the government, other protests would champion an even more abstract cause: community. This cause would prove to be a very hard sell when pitted against Hong Kong's pro-property developer bias.

In 2003, the Urban Renewal Authority, or URA, announced a major redevelopment of the Lee Tung Street area in Wan Chai. Lee Tung Street was also known as 'Wedding Card Street' thanks to the proliferation of traditional wedding invitation printers located in the ground floor shopfronts of the street's tenement buildings. Among the many property development projects in Hong Kong's constantly-shifting cityscape, the redevelopment of Wedding Card Street may have attracted attention in particular due to the cultural significance wedding cards represented. Wedding cards in Hong Kong are the first public expression of a couple's commitment to one another. The intricately-designed red and gold leaf invitation cards with traditional Chinese designs are hand-delivered by the couple or their parents, a sign of respect signifying the value the couple and their families place on each recipient's blessing of the marriage.[10]

Ironically, it was the government that first required the printing shops to be congregated along Lee Tung Street, where officials could more readily keep an eye on them to prevent counterfeiting. In the 1970s, the street's printing stores made a simple trade in calendars and promotional wedding invitations for restaurants. The area's fame grew as Hong Kong's economy boomed in the 1980s and increasingly wealthy couples demanded more elaborate wedding cards.

In 2003, however, the government was ready for the printers to move on. The URA said the proposed redevelopment project would 'regenerate the Wan Chai old town into a new precinct of leisure, shopping, residential and commercial activities'.[11] The URA estimated that 930 households and 2000 residents would be affected by the redevelopment plan, which called for the demolition of the entire existing neighbourhood and the construction of a new mixed-use, high-end retail and residential complex. Unspoken was the fact that this significant chunk of prime real estate in one of Hong Kong's busiest neighbourhoods was being under-utilised by low-rise tenement buildings, and that constructing a high-rise, high-density development would generate significant profits for the government and its private developer partners.

The plan immediately attracted criticism from residents and heritage activists who were concerned not only with retaining the traditional character of the area, but also with preserving the existing social networks of the neighbourhood and its residents. More than one-third of the neighbourhood's residents were over sixty years old, and two-thirds had owned their properties for over twenty years.[12] It was unlikely that they would be able to afford apartments in the towering new luxury development.

Long-term resident May Je was one of the leaders of a local group formed to protest the development. May Je had owned a wedding dress shop on the street for almost twenty years, and recalled the district's community spirit. For instance, people living in the buildings would gather to share both meals and supplies. Fellow activist Mrs Kam had lived in the street almost her entire life. Her father had started his business on Lee Tung Street in the 1970s, and Mrs Kam had worked in the store since she was a young girl. Mr Chin Kam-piu, owner of a number of printing shops on the street, pointed out that the hard-won fame of Wedding Card Street could not be easily replicated in another location. 'No promotion is needed for printing shops in this street. Business comes naturally. With years of hard work, we made the street famous – everybody comes here for their wedding cards,' Mr Chin explained.[13]

The redevelopment would uproot people like May Je, Mrs Kam and Mr Chin and destroy their community.

In an attempt to address the heritage concerns, the

URA announced that the redevelopment would include a 'Wedding City'-themed area. Wedding-related shops and businesses would be given priority in leasing retail spaces and the development would include 'Hong Kong's first wedding traditions and culture gallery'.[14] However, these concessions did not address the concerns about the neighbourhood's imperilled social networks and community.

Activists initially tried to work within the system, appealing to the URA, appearing before LegCo committees and submitting their own alternative development proposal to the Town Planning Board. However, the Town Planning Board rejected the activists' proposal and the redevelopment proceeded with only minor concessions. In the words of one activist: '[We] came to the conclusion that no matter how we tried to appear moderate and followed the rules of the game, the game would only be unfair under the existing institutional arrangements.'[15]

So the activists turned to protest. They marched on government headquarters and disrupted Town Planning Board meetings. As demolition got underway, protesters entered the site and attempted to block workers from commencing the job. Some activists, including May Je and Mrs Kam, began a hunger strike. Ultimately, the protesters were unsuccessful, undone partly by their own lack of unity. Unlike Star Ferry and Queen's Piers, which were public buildings, Lee Tung Street involved private property, and some of the property owners had already accepted the government's compensation. Thus, the government argued that it would be unfair to accept the activists' alternative development proposal and break deals that had already been reached with those owners.

The failure of the protest revealed that when heritage is pitted against commercial interests, heritage always loses. In 2015, the new development opened to the public, revealing a clinical, modern retail development devoid of the local character of Wedding Card Street, the old printing stores replaced with high end boutiques and an outlet of an international café chain.

*

Concerns about the environment, community and undemocratic decision-making processes came together in the dispute over the Hong Kong to Guangzhou high speed rail project and the demolition of Choi Yuen Tsuen village.[16] As far back as 2000, the Hong Kong government had been considering proposals to build an express rail link connecting Hong Kong to the Mainland's railway system, reducing travel times between Hong Kong and Guangzhou to under an hour. By 2008, a formal proposal was put forward to construct a

26-kilometre-long section of express rail through Hong Kong, terminating in West Kowloon, alongside the new West Kowloon Cultural District. The proposal would require the demolition and relocation of the village of Choi Yuen Tsuen in rural Yuen Long. The villagers initially protested the plan, with little success. However, in 2009, their cause attracted the attention of young activists who had been engaged in the Star Ferry and Queen's Pier protest campaigns. The youth, led by among others activist Eddie Chu Hoi-dick and his group Local Action, were concerned not only at the environmental damage and the disruption to the Choi Yuen Tsuen community which the project posed, but also that yet another project was being forced upon the community with inadequate consultation and through an undemocratic process.

These young activists joined forces with the villagers, forming the Choi Yuen Tsuen Support Group. They found a sympathetic ear from pan-democrat legislators who were increasingly concerned at poor government oversight and the project's ballooning budget, and sought to block the project. While the pan-democrat legislators worked to filibuster and derail proceedings within the LegCo building in early 2010, the protesters surrounded the building outside. The protesters adopted a 'kow-towing' form of protest, which involved walking slowly and prostrating themselves on the ground every

26 steps (representing the 26 kilometres of railway), a form of protest directly inspired by the Korean farmers' Anti-WTO protests in 2005. Pro-Beijing legislators finally pushed the funding proposal for the project through LegCo's finance committee, although they were forced to remain barricaded inside for hours afterwards while protesters continued to besiege the building. After violent clashes, the protesters were finally dispersed by police late into the night.

The high speed rail project remained under construction in 2016, and the budget had continued to balloon. The government forced an additional HKD19.6 billion of funding for the project through the LegCo finance committee in March 2016, prompting further protests inside the LegCo chamber by pan-democrat legislators, with 'Long Hair' Leung throwing ink at the pro-Beijing committee chairman in frustration.[17]

After the village of Choi Yuen Tsuen was destroyed and the villagers relocated, Eddie Chu and his newly established Land Justice League worked with the villagers to establish a sustainable farming project in Pak Heung.[18] Meanwhile, Chu continued to campaign for pro-environment, anti-property-development causes and to push for greater transparency and fairness in land use and development policies.

*

The Wedding Card Street protests and other 'heritage protests' of this era were arguing against the inevitability that everything has an expiry date in Hong Kong. This point was made poignantly by film-maker Wong Kar-Wai in his classic of Hong Kong cinema, *Chungking Express*, in which he compared fading love to an expiring tin of pineapple. 'Somehow everything comes with an expiry date,' muses his lovelorn character He Qiwu, 'If memories could be canned would they also have expiry dates?' Activists' concerns stemmed from a desire to ensure that Hong Kong's distinct identity – an identity contained within the collective memories surrounding these heritage sites and communities – did not expire along with those memories.

This identity was perceived as being under threat, not only by destruction from within but also by encroachment from across the border. As Hong Kong's economic importance to Mainland China waned, Beijing became emboldened. The central government saw that a key path to shaping the territory according to its vision would be through influencing future generations of Hong Kongers. Then-President Hu Jintao stated during a 2007 visit to Hong Kong: '[Y]oung people . . . represent the future of Hong Kong . . . We should foster a strong sense of national identity among the young people in Hong Kong . . . so that they will carry forward the Hong Kong people's great tradition of "loving the motherland and loving Hong

Kong".[19] The Hong Kong government's policy-attempt to meet Hu's exhortation would provoke yet another large-scale – and this time successful – protest.

In May 2011, the Curriculum Development Council recommended that a compulsory 'Moral and National Education' civics course be introduced into all Hong Kong schools. When an Education Bureau-supported organisation released a proposed curriculum in July 2012 entitled 'The China Model', there was widespread alarm at its contents. Critics argued that the curriculum was akin to 'brainwashing'. The China Model curriculum praised the benefits of Leninist-style 'democratic centralism', criticised the notion of 'Western self-defined universal values of freedom and democracy' and described Western multi-party politics as a 'fierce inter-party rivalry that makes the people suffer'.[20]

Parents as well as teachers and students were outraged at what they saw as biased, inaccurate information about the Mainland and sycophantic praise of the central government, with no encouragement of independent or critical thinking. In response, a group of secondary school students led by fifteen-year-old Joshua Wong founded an activist group called Scholarism. Scholarism, with the support of the National Education Parents' Concern Group and the Professional Teachers' Union, led a campaign against the National Education plan. At the end of July 2011, 90 000 people protested against the plan.[21] Protesters, including many parents with young children, dressed in black and waved banners as they marched. Students wore red blindfolds and chanted: 'No brainwashing!' The march ended at Tamar Park outside the government headquarters in Admiralty, where the protesters settled in for an extended occupation, with concerts and rallies continuing over the next several months. The protests were very much driven by the students themselves, with Wong and others from Scholarism leading rallies and acting as spokespeople.

The response to the protests from Wong Chi Man, who directed the National Education Services Centre responsible for the China Model curriculum, was hardly encouraging. 'All education is, to some extent, designed to brainwash,' he stated.[22] An official from the Central Government Liaison Office, Beijing's representative office in Hong Kong concurred, calling national education 'necessary brainwashing'.[23]

In August, three members of Scholarism began a hunger strike at Civic Square, outside the entrance to the government headquarters. The protests spread to university campuses, with university students boycotting their classes and staging a sit-in outside Chief Executive C.Y. Leung's home. In September, as the new school year approached, an additional public protest involving 120 000 people was held outside government headquarters.

In the face of this overwhelming public opposition – and perhaps to stem the bad PR associated with images of hunger-striking schoolchildren – the government relented and announced that the Moral and National Education subject would no longer be compulsory, leaving schools free to decide whether or not to implement the programme. It also withdrew the curriculum guide entirely, freeing schools which chose to teach the Moral and National Education course to adopt any teaching materials they felt appropriate.[24] Following this victory, Scholarism remained active, campaigning for other political and social causes. The organisation was to become a key participant in the Umbrella Movement.

*

While some of the protests of the 2000s were successful, many failed to achieve their goals. These failures convinced activists that it was not only Hong Kong's unsentimental 'development at all costs' ethos that was the problem, but also the imbalanced governance system in which corporate and business interests were privileged by the LegCo functional constituency system and the chief executive election committee. It was clear that the government remained free to pursue any policy agenda it chose regardless of media outcry or public opinion, provided that it had the support of economic and social elites.

The heritage campaigns served not only as an assertion of Hong Kong identity in the face of perceived incursions, but also – especially insofar as the protesters voiced objections to an unfair and undemocratic system – as an impetus for political change. This growing impetus would, a few years later, prompt the beginning of the Umbrella Movement, the ultimate – if temporary – victory for citizens in their battle for public space.

V

The Umbrella Movement

In 1984, while David Wilson secured elections for LegCo, the best promise he was able to extract regarding the chief executive was that election by universal suffrage was the 'ultimate aim'.[1] In the meantime, the chief executive would be selected by a small group of largely pro-Beijing politicians and business elites, with Beijing indicating that universal suffrage would be adopted for the chief executive elections in 2017.

'Universal suffrage' was expected to give all Hong Kongers the right to vote for the chief executive. However, it remained unclear how candidates for that election would be *nominated*. Many of Hong Kong's pan-democrat politicians had hoped for a mechanism for 'civil nomination', whereby anyone could be nominated as a candidate to participate in the election. The democrats recognised that, as long as candidates were still nominated by a Beijing-controlled nominating committee, none of their own would ever be able to enter the race.

However, as the time approached for Beijing's official decision on the chief executive election process, which was to be announced in 2014, all indications seemed to suggest that Beijing was not in an accommodating mood.

On 10 June 2014, China's State Council (broadly equivalent to a cabinet) issued a white paper entitled 'The Practice of the "One Country, Two Systems" Policy in the Hong Kong Special Administrative Region'.[2] The white paper purported to promote a 'comprehensive and correct understanding and implementation' of the 'One Country, Two Systems policy' in Hong Kong and reflected the latest in official thinking in Beijing towards the governance of Hong Kong. The white paper was controversial in its emphasis of the 'One Country' over the 'Two Systems'. The autonomy promised to Hong Kong under the Sino-British Joint Declaration and the Basic Law, it stated, was not without limits: 'The high degree of autonomy of HKSAR is not an inherent power, but one that comes solely from the authorization by the central leadership . . . It is the power to run local affairs as authorized by the central leadership.'[3]

The white paper also stirred discord in Hong Kong's

legal community with its characterisation of judges as 'administrators', for whom, as for other civil servants, 'loving the country is the basic political requirement'. The statement led to a sharp rebuke from Hong Kong's Bar Council.[4] When the president of the Law Society (which represents Hong Kong's solicitors) made conciliatory statements in support of the white paper, he was promptly forced by his fellow members of the profession to resign.[5]

Anger at the white paper spurred the largest 1 July protest since 2004, with 166 000 marchers.[6] The protest ended in Central with an all-night student sit-in around a replica model of Tiananmen Square's Goddess of Democracy and a large 'white paper' tank.

Thus, in early summer 2014, as all awaited Beijing's decision on the chief executive election reforms, Hong Kong simmered in an atmosphere of mistrust and discontent with the Mainland, as well as what many saw as its enablers in Hong Kong – Chief Executive C.Y. Leung and his administration. Leung was an extremely unpopular figure, with approval ratings even lower than those of the ill-fated Tung Chee-Hwa. It was hard to tell what Hong Kongers objected to more, his authoritarian approach and seeming insensitivity to public sentiment or the persistent rumours that Leung had long been a secret member of the Chinese Communist Party – a charge he consistently denied.

This discontent also focused public attention on a proposal by a hitherto little-known Hong Kong legal academic. As early as January 2013, Benny Tai Yiu-ting, an academic in the faculty of law at the University of Hong Kong, proposed that – if the electoral reforms did not meet Hong Kong's expectations – there should be an act of 'civil disobedience' to protest.[7] In his proposal, Tai evoked the same spirit of Gandhi's non-violent resistance that had inspired So Sau-chung in his protest against the Star Ferry Company in 1966.

Tai, together with his collaborators Chan Kin-man, a Chinese University of Hong Kong academic, and Reverend Chu Yiu-ming, a Baptist minister, formed a group called 'Occupy Central With Love and Peace' to organise the protest.[8] Tai proposed a sit-in in Hong Kong's Central business district during the 1 October National Day holiday. The Occupy Central group expected to stage their sit-in, be symbolically arrested at the end of their day of peaceful resistance and raise awareness for the democratic cause.

When China's parliament, the National People's Congress, announced the electoral reforms on 31 August 2014, the changes were, unsurprisingly, a disappointment to Hong Kong's democrats.[9] Beijing proposed that the following mechanism be adopted for the election of Hong Kong's next chief executive:

- A 'nominating committee' would be formed, similar to the current election committee.
- The nominating committee would nominate only two to three candidates (more candidates than that would 'confuse' voters, said Beijing officials).
- Each candidate would need to receive the endorsement of more than half of the nominating committee (a higher bar than the current 150 of 1200 members required for nomination).
- All eligible Hong Kong electors would then vote to elect one of the candidates as chief executive.

It was a process clearly designed to ensure that only Beijing-approved candidates could run for the office. In response to this disappointing decision, the Occupy Central group confirmed that they would go ahead with their protest during the October holiday.

Leading up to Tai's proposed protest, a group of students led by the Hong Kong Federation of Students, or HKFS (an alliance of university student unions), and Joshua Wong's Scholarism staged a week-long class boycott. The week of protest culminated on the night of Friday, 26 September, when students stormed Civic Square, the site of Scholarism's successful protest against the National Education Curriculum two years earlier. After the government and police closed Civic Square off to all public access, a group of students led by Wong and

HKFS leader Lester Shum scaled the fence and commenced a sit-in. The sit-in carried into Saturday night, and the crowds grew as many members of the local community came down to support the students.

On the morning of Sunday, 28 September, Benny Tai formally announced what many had already recognised as the reality: 'Occupy Central' had begun, several days earlier than expected, and at the government headquarters in Admiralty instead of in Central.

As word of Tai's announcement spread, more supporters began to converge on Admiralty to join the protests. Police formed a cordon around the site to prevent the crowds from growing. They also detained a number of pan-democrat politicians as they attempted to bring equipment and supplies to the site. However, the police cordon proved counterproductive as the crowds grew, spilling over onto the road and quickly flooding eight lanes of the highway. Soon, traffic came to a standstill.

The crowds continued to push up against the police line, attempting to join their fellow protesters on the other side of the barriers. Police repelled them with pepper spray and then, when that had no effect, suddenly and without warning, with tear gas. Hong Kongers watching the events live on television and online were outraged. This was a level of police violence not seen in Hong Kong since the 1967 riots. What's more, it seemed

Protesters with their umbrellas unfurled face the police line in Mong Kok, October 2014

disproportionate to the actions of the crowds, who were armed only with umbrellas and cling film to deflect the pepper spray. As a result, more protesters flocked to the site to lend their support.

Contrary to police expectations, the crowds in Admiralty were getting larger, not dispersing. The protesters remained peaceful, sitting on the road facing the riot police and singing a popular Canto-pop hit by Hong Kong band Beyond, 'Under A Vast Sky'. The tune would become the unofficial theme song of the movement.

At the same time, spontaneous 'occupations' broke out in other key locations in the city: the Causeway Bay shopping district, the tourist hub Tsim Sha Tsui and the working class Mong Kok district. It quickly became apparent that police simply did not have sufficient ranks

Protesters post a banner reading: 'I want genuine universal suffrage', September 2014

to clear all the roads, and so they retreated, ceding the streets to protesters.

In subsequent days, even as the government attempted to soothe public outrage by announcing that the riot police had been withdrawn, massive daily protests continued, with crowds easily numbering in the hundreds of thousands. The atmosphere was jubilant, the crowd overwhelmingly young: university students and high school students all wearing black, except for those who came directly from school still wearing their uniforms. This was the generation that arguably had the greatest stake in the issue at hand: Hong Kong's future.

The protests quickly fostered a remarkable sense of community. Protesters and their supporters distributed free water, food and supplies, established first aid stations and lending libraries, collected rubbish and sorted it for recycling and still found time to do their homework. Volunteers gave public lectures, and there were spontaneous discussion groups and nightly 'sharing sessions' where people gathered to discuss their thoughts and feelings on the day's events.

The student protesters announced four key demands:

1. Chief Executive C.Y. Leung should resign.
2. The NPC decision on chief executive elections should be revoked.
3. A new election process should be proposed, allowing for 'civil nomination' of candidates.
4. 'Genuine universal suffrage' should be implemented.

As the protests continued, the government refused to engage in discussions with the protesters, perhaps calculating that their best strategy was to wait out the protests until fatigue and a creeping lack of interest reduced the numbers, and police could then sweep up any stragglers. However, towards the end of the second week of protests, Chief Secretary Carrie Lam made the mistake of publicly observing that protester numbers were dwindling, and the protests losing support.

In response, Joshua Wong and his fellow student leaders called for their supporters to bring tents and 'move in' to what would soon be called Harcourt Village, to occupy the roads permanently until the government made the demanded concessions. 'You know what to do!' declared Wong. 'Make Harcourt Road our home!'[10] Within days, a tent city sprang up in the three occupied zones, blocking many kilometres of the city's main arterial roads. A tent census at the peak of the occupation recorded over 2000 tents in Admiralty alone, with hundreds more in Mong Kok and Causeway Bay.

The infrastructure in Harcourt Village became more entrenched by the day. Carpenters helped to build increasingly sophisticated staircases over the cement road barriers. Makeshift 'shower' tents were set up. The public bathrooms were regularly cleaned by volunteers and equipped with an impressively comprehensive selection of free toiletries.

There was also the 'Homework Zone', to the delight and fascination of many. The Homework Zone began when a volunteer carpenter hammered together some planks to make a few desks over a traffic barrier so that students would have a more comfortable place to study. From there it grew, with more furniture being constructed every day. Marquees were pitched above the desks to protect students from the elements. Then carpet was laid down, and a diesel generator installed to light night-time study sessions and facilitate free Wi-Fi. Volunteers provided tutoring, with a sign posted advising which tutors were on duty.

By mid-October, the Admiralty protest site had come to resemble nothing so much as an outdoor community arts festival. After emphasising in the initial days of the protest that this was a serious matter and 'not a carnival', student organisers finally relented and began to publish a programme for the coming days' activities, including guest speakers, movie screenings and live bands. On the mild and sunny autumn weekends, thousands flocked with their families to visit the site. There was a constant variety of spontaneous events: free portrait sketching, leather work, weaving and origami (making paper umbrellas, of course). Musicians played impromptu gigs: a young singer and guitarist named Bananaooyoo was a crowd favourite, giving nightly performances as people rushed to catch the last train home. Dancers performed routines, invariably involving umbrellas.

The Umbrella Movement protests prompted an outpouring of creativity, achieving in a matter of weeks more than the government's Leisure and Cultural Services Department had been able to achieve through years of arts initiatives. The site was plastered with posters, banners, flyers, graffiti, paintings, sculptures and installations. This was replicated online, too, with a constant stream of cartoons, photos, memes and online humour shared in response to the latest events.

Art students from Hong Kong Baptist University created a patchwork canopy made from discarded umbrellas damaged by pepper spray and tear gas. The canopy was suspended over the main stage set up at the centre of the protest site – a stretch of Harcourt Road renamed 'Umbrella Square' – to shade speakers and audiences from the sun.

Umbrella Man, a monumental wooden statue over two metres high that took the form of a man holding aloft a yellow umbrella, was wheeled into Umbrella Square. The statue, created by local Hong Kong artist Milk, recalled an image captured during the early days of the protests of a protester holding his umbrella to shelter a police officer during a rainstorm.

But the most striking art installation of them all was the Lennon Wall. It began with a simple gesture: at the bottom of a plain concrete staircase, winding its way down the outside of the government headquarters building, someone put up a poster posing the question: Why are we here? With the poster was a small supply of sticky notes and felt-tip pens. The multi-hued sticky notes quickly multiplied as both locals and visitors left messages of support, encouragement and defiance. The notes grew to cover the entire length of wall, a dense rainbow of yellow, pink, orange and blue, running up ten metres of staircase and fluttering in the breeze. At night, the Lennon Wall glowed under the perpetually lit fluorescent tubes, a beacon in the night. Nearby, a computer was set up to project onto the wall messages of support submitted via a website from well-wishers around the world. The messages came from Vancouver and London, from the Ukraine and Gaza and even Prague, home of the Lennon Wall's namesake.

The protesters' greatest public victory came almost a month into the protests on 21 October, when the government agreed to participate in a televised debate with student leaders. Not only did this give the protesters and their movement legitimacy, it also gave them the opportunity to argue their case directly to the government as equals. Big screens were set up in the protest zones on the night of the debate, and large crowds gathered to watch and cheer on the students.

The contrast between the two sides was striking. The five government representatives, appointed bureaucrats among which all but one had never faced an election, were wooden and mechanical, putting on a performance that did nothing to ameliorate the image of a government out of touch with its people. The student leaders, on the other hand, were real politicians, having earned their places at the table through student union elections. They appeared in their signature black T-shirts facing off against the stiff bureaucrats, a clear echo of the televised appearance of Tiananmen student protesters meeting with Li Peng and other Chinese government leaders in 1989.[11] The students spoke with passion, conviction and humour. What's more, they spoke not only about the narrow political and constitutional issues that had previously been their primary agenda, but also articulated broader social concerns – income inequality, housing affordability, the influence of tycoons in Hong Kong. These were concerns that had a direct impact on the lives of ordinary Hong Kongers; the students clearly won the night.

Unfortunately, the debate did not result in further talks between the government and protesters, and the protests stretched into November with little progress made. By mid-November, time finally seemed to be running out for the protesters: a number of taxi and minibus companies successfully took action in the Hong Kong High Court to obtain injunctions, requiring protesters to clear blockaded roads in the occupied areas and authorising bailiffs to request police assistance in enforcing the injunctions.

The court ruling did not change the legal position of the protesters. Their protests already constituted 'unlawful assemblies' under the Public Order Ordinance, and the protesters could have been arrested at any time. What the court ruling did do, however, was provide political cover for the government. Now, clearing the protesters by force could be justified with appeals to the importance of upholding the 'rule of law', a Hong Kong Core Value competing for legitimacy with the Core Values promoted by the ongoing protest. This attempt to force a legal solution to a political problem was clearly unsatisfactory, and the government's use of 'rule of law' as justification for this action after weeks of inaction appeared hypocritical and disingenuous.

As police clear the Mong Kok protest site, a protester anticipates violence with a home-made shield reading: 'Police remain calm', November 2014

At the end of November, police supported bailiffs in executing the injunction against the Mong Kok protest site on Nathan Road, and the site was cleared. A week later, on 9 December, a police spokesperson announced at the end of a routine press conference that the Admiralty protest site would also be cleared, 'to re-open the blocked roads so that the general public can resume their normal daily lives'.[12]

This was the end.

Thousands turned out at the main Admiralty protest site for what would be the last night in Umbrella Square. It was a night filled with nostalgia. Visitors posed for photographs and collected keepsakes. Parents brought their children, with one parent commenting: 'I want them to see this, and remember it, so they know what Hong Kongers are capable of.'[13] Meanwhile, protesters started the process of packing up, removing supplies and dismantling tents.

At the steps of the Admiralty subway station exit, Bananaooyoo set up his guitar and microphone to play the last of his nightly gigs. As he sang the theme songs of the movement, the audience joined in, tears in their eyes.

Late in the night, archivists begin dismantling the Lennon Wall, photographing it section by section and then removing each colourful note carefully, collating and storing them in archive boxes.

The following day, police and government contractors moved in to clear the main Umbrella Square site. They worked their way through the protest zone, dismantling tents, tearing down banners and posters, stacking all the debris into piles. The police riot squad laid into the abandoned Homework Zone and made quick work of it; the homemade wooden furniture was heaped into a pile like so much firewood. Knives slashed through tarpaulins and tents, and, in just a few minutes, the

'Homework Zone' was gone. Dump trucks and cleaners followed behind the police, sweeping everything up.

Meanwhile, a curious assembly of young and old gathered on the roadside next to an adjacent freeway overpass. This group of over 200 people – staging a symbolic final sit-in in defiance of police orders to clear the site – included members of HKFS and Scholarism, as well as senior democratic politician all-stars, among them founding chairman of the Democratic Party Martin Lee, founding leader of the Civic Party Audrey Eu, radical legislator 'Long Hair' Leung, media mogul Jimmy Lai and chairwoman of the Democratic Party, Emily Lau. As these veterans sat on the asphalt shoulder-to-shoulder with the students, everyone patiently awaiting arrest, it appeared that a torch was being passed from one generation to the next.

Lau, a stalwart of Hong Kong's democratic politics, explained that Hong Kong's youth had not always been so engaged. 'We've been struggling for democracy for several decades,' she said, 'but very few young people took part. Most of them did not register as voters, and even if they did register many of them did not bother to vote. They just thought that the whole thing had nothing to do with them.'[14]

The Umbrella Movement gave Lau some cause for optimism: 'I hope this whole experience will be with them for the rest of their lives, and that they will inject a lot of vigour into the pro-democracy movement.' However, Lau warned that the younger generation needed to engage in the mainstream political process to take their movement forward: 'I hope these young people can channel their energy into the electoral system as well, and think about forming or joining political parties. They will have to learn that the movement is more than just demonstrations in the streets.'[15]

But was Lau right? Past experiences in Hong Kong had shown that 'demonstrations in the streets' were indeed a more effective means of achieving change in Hong Kong than participating in the political system. This may have been the inconvenient truth behind a remarkable public opinion poll conducted by Hong Kong University in the midst of the protests, which found that HKFS (which is not a political party) was Hong Kong's most supported political group, outpolling Lau's own Democratic Party.[16]

In the case of the Umbrella Movement, however, Lau was proven right. The demonstrations had come to an end. After a long day sitting on the road, Lau and 207 others were eventually arrested that night. All were released without charge the following morning.

By nightfall, the kilometre-long stretch of highway that had been home to the protesters for seventy-five days had been swept clean; traffic flowed where rows of colourful tents, banners and hand-made wooden furniture had stood only hours earlier. With the clearance of the small protest site in the Causeway Bay shopping district the following Monday, the protests were officially over.

*

On its face, the Umbrella Movement was a failure. Beijing and its representative in Hong Kong, C.Y. Leung, did not budge on any of the protesters' demands. One of the fundamental flaws of the protests was their insistence on these core demands, when clearly none of them would ever be acceptable to Beijing. Leung could not resign. After the resignation of inaugural chief executive Tung Chee-Hwa in the wake of the 1 July 2003 and 2004 protests, losing a second chief executive in similar circumstances would be unacceptable to Beijing. Nor would the Mainland government make any concessions in the chief executive election process, which had already been very publicly decided by the National People's Congress. The loss of face would be unthinkable.

The nature of the protest movement itself also precluded any negotiation towards a mutually acceptable outcome. The protest groups were heterogeneous and without centralised leadership; even if the student groups leading the Admiralty-based occupation agreed to retreat, there was no assurance that protesters in Mong Kok would agree to do likewise.

Indeed, the movement was arguably a failure before it had even begun. Tai stated in early September, prior to the Umbrella Movement's launch, that his initial threat to 'occupy' the city had been intended to put pressure on Beijing in advance of their decision on universal suffrage. When the disappointing decision was handed down in August, Tai conceded that his threat had not been effective.[17]

However, political reform was only one of Tai's goals. The other was 'social awakening', a goal he said after the Umbrella Movement had concluded that was achieved 'far more than was intended'.[18] So the continuation of the occupation even after it became apparent

As the Admiralty occupied site is cleared, the Lennon Wall is adorned with a message to the future: 'Even if disappointed, don't despair', December 2014

that the government would not cave in to the protesters' demands became an important means of extending and promoting this social awakening, while solidifying a new collective identity among Hong Kongers.

The extended occupation also helped to show the importance of the younger generation to Hong Kong politics, and of grassroots organisations and horizontal networks rather than top-down political structures. These may have had the opportunity to develop further if not for the fact that, in some ways, the movement was a victim of its own success. As HKFS leader Nathan Law explained: 'The reaction from the public at the start of the movement surprised us. We didn't take time to think about strategy, whether reducing the occupied areas or retreating or otherwise.'[19]

The scale of the initial occupation exceeded protest leaders' expectations to such an extent that they had no strategy to cope with it, and never developed one. They never planned on being allowed to stay for so long, as days of government inaction turned into weeks and then months. So in many ways, the final clearance brought relief for the protesters and authorities alike.

The government's constitutional reform bill – in the form initially proposed by Beijing – was presented to LegCo in June 2015. Using the slogan 'Pocket it now', the administration had spent the prior months trying to convince Hong Kongers that 'something is better than nothing', hardly an inspiring message to sell to an already jaded and exhausted populace.

The pan-democrats were steadfast in their determination to vote against the bill. However, in the final result they did not even have to exercise their veto. In an embarrassing fiasco, the pro-Beijing parties, led by the Democratic Alliance for the Betterment and Progress of Hong Kong, bungled an attempt to stage a walkout in the LegCo chamber in order to break quorum and stall the voting. They miscounted, the vote went ahead and in the end attracted only eight votes in favour. All of the pan-democrat legislators voted against the bill, and the bill failed to pass.

Hong Kong remains stalled on its road to universal suffrage. In 2017, the twentieth anniversary of the handover, a new chief executive was chosen for Hong Kong – not by a vote of the people, but again by a vote of the 1200 professional and business elites comprising the election committee. It came as little surprise that their choice was Carrie Lam Cheng Yuet-ngor, chief secretary under C.Y. Leung and Beijing's anointed candidate.

The Umbrella Movement was the zenith of the previous fifty years of protest in Hong Kong. The imagery of police raising their black warning banners and firing tear gas into crowds of protesters recalled images of the 1967 riots. The anxiety over the encroaching threat of undemocratic Mainland politics was the continuation of a struggle for Hong Kong values that began in the 1980s and '90s after the signing of the Joint Declaration and the 4 June Tiananmen incident. The belief in the effectiveness of protest to attract the attention of Beijing and seek a change in policy, if not leadership, drew on the lessons of the protests of 1 July 2003 and 2004. The Hong Kong heritage protests of the 2000s gave protesters the opportunity to hone their protest strategy and build a community of activists supported by a diverse range of civil society groups – the same community that sustained the Umbrella Movement throughout its seventy-eight-day occupation of Hong Kong's streets.

While the longed-for universal suffrage has not yet been achieved, the Umbrella Movement protesters' voices have been heard clearly, not just by Beijing but also by fellow citizens. This may prove to be the enduring success of the movement. Many protesters spoke of realising for the first time that they were not alone in their concern about these political issues. The resulting community that grew up around the movement has so far proven to be resilient, forming the ideological basis for a series of ongoing protests, new civil society groups and even new political parties. Scholarism announced its dissolution in early 2016, and its members, including Joshua Wong and HKFS leader Nathan Law, formed a new political party. That party, Demosistō, together with another youth party inspired by the Umbrella Movement, Youngspiration, contested the LegCo elections in 2016, with Law and two members of Youngspiration successfully winning seats – a stunning result for the political newcomers and a sharp rebuke to those who argued that the Umbrella Movement had achieved nothing. In another notable link between political protest and the 2016 LegCo election, Eddie Chu, veteran of the Star Ferry and high speed rail protests, running with his land justice, anti-property-development platform, successfully won a seat and also attracted the highest number of votes of any single candidate.[20]

The record turnout for the 2016 elections – 58 per cent of registered voters participated, a historic high eclipsing even the election of 2004 which came in the aftermath of the Article 23 protests – was clear evidence that the Umbrella Movement had energised political participation among Hong Kong's populace.[21] The Umbrella Movement also served as a model for new forms of political engagement through broad community participation in artistic expression, performances and debates. Many of the artists who gained prominence during the Umbrella Movement have continued to find an audience and a following in subsequent years, making ongoing contributions to the cultural life of the city.

Finally, the Umbrella Movement served to politicise a generation of youth in Hong Kong and demolished the myth that Hong Kong people – in particular young people – do not care about politics. The Umbrella Movement protesters showed with their bodies, by sleeping on concrete for weeks, by putting themselves in the path of pepper spray and police batons, that they care deeply about their home, about their identity and about their communities. The protests are sure to be remembered as the formative event for an entire generation of Hong Kongers, many of whom will be future leaders and set the tone for public debate – and protest – in Hong Kong for decades to come.

VI

Towards 2047

The Umbrella Movement protests made clear that the Hong Kong people are in an unusual predicament. If they are unhappy with government policy, they are neither able to 'vote out' the government nor to participate meaningfully in the policy-making process. However, Hong Kong does continue to enjoy the freedoms of expression and assembly, among other fundamental rights and freedoms guaranteed by the Basic Law and the Bill of Rights Ordinance.

This combination, described by former Governor Chris Patten as 'liberty without democracy',[1] is unique. Most countries without democratic elections also circumscribe assembly and free speech, so that public protest is not possible. Under an authoritarian regime, you can't vote out the government, but you are also not permitted to criticise or protest against it. Likewise, most places in the world that enjoy free assembly, free speech and other rights and freedoms do so within the context of a broader system of representative democracy, such that protest is but one of a variety of forms of political participation available to citizens.

Hong Kong, however, finds itself in a state of disequilibrium: the city's precarious balancing of a high level of freedom against a low level of representative democracy is not a natural state. While some may point out that this had always been the case in Hong Kong, this arrangement was arguably viable in Hong Kong prior to the 1997 handover because the ultimate sovereign, the United Kingdom, was itself a democratic multi-party state, subject to the inherent checks and balances of that system, monitored by an independent media and ultimately accountable to a voting public – even if this voting public was not the same public that was being governed in Hong Kong.[2] There is a degree of comfort to be found in the thought that, in the event of a despotic use of power, there exists a mechanism for change, no matter how remote. However, in the post-handover years with the ultimate sovereign power being replaced with a single-party dictatorship, the imbalance has shown itself to be increasingly unsustainable, and Hong Kong has seen mounting pressure to right it.

The Umbrella Movement of 2014 and other recent protests have aimed to address the disequilibrium by pushing for increased representative democracy. Since the Umbrella Movement, diverse groups have become increasingly active in making demands that range along a spectrum from, at the more moderate end, less Mainland interference in Hong Kong to, at its most extreme, full independence. These 'localist' groups have received particular support from Hong Kong's youth who are frustrated with the apparent ineffectiveness of the pan-democrat professional politicians and are demanding more radical action. Indeed, one of the hallmarks of the post-Umbrella Movement era has been this increase in radical politics as well as increasing fragmentation among the traditional pro-democracy camp, often along generational lines. A 'new era of civil disobedience' in Hong Kong has seemingly arrived, promoted by this newly emergent localist movement.[3]

The years after the Umbrella Movement have seen increasingly frequent protests in Hong Kong, many with an 'anti-Mainland' slant. In towns near the Shenzhen border, protesters rallied against traders from the Mainland who were said to be flooding local shopping districts to make bulk purchases of medicines, milk powder and other products whose Mainland purveyors are viewed with mistrust. Protesters decried the fact that these traders were squeezing out small local businesses in the process. Others protested against the 'Dancing Aunties', middle-aged Mainland Chinese women who gather in Mong Kok to sing and dance to Chinese revolutionary music, blasted through loudspeakers at a disturbingly high volume.[4] And in a more unusual expression of 'anti-Mainland' sentiment, protesters marched on the Japanese consulate to protest a change of the Chinese name for the Pokémon character Pikachu from a Cantonese transliteration to a Mandarin one. Pokémon in its Cantonese form, protesters argued, was another part of Hong Kong's collective memory.[5]

Other protests have been directed at the police, including protests against perceived abuses of police powers and in support of arrested protesters. One particularly notable protest concerned a female protester who alleged that a police officer sexually assaulted her. The woman was subsequently charged and convicted of assaulting a police officer with her breast. 'Breasts are not weapons,' chanted the protesters who gathered outside Hong Kong's High Court to mock the decision.[6]

By far the most serious of these incidents occurred in Mong Kok on Chinese New Year's day, 8 February 2016, in what came to be known as the 'Fishball Riot' – the worst violence seen in Hong Kong's streets since the riots of 1966 and 1967.[7] Once again, concerns about local culture and heritage combined with political issues to precipitate protest.

The Lunar New Year street market is a long-standing Chinese tradition, and Hong Kong authorities had traditionally turned a blind eye to unlicensed street vendors selling local snacks such as fishballs and stinky tofu during the festive season. However, on this occasion, officers from Hong Kong's Food and Environmental Hygiene Department attempted to shut down the vendors, prompting activists led by localist group Hong Kong Indigenous to put out a call for supporters to convene in Mong Kok and 'protect' the vendors. This in turn led to confrontations between the officers and protesters, and police were called in to break up the scuffles. As more protesters and more police flocked to the area, the scene quickly degenerated into violence and rioting.

Protesters and police engaged in confrontations with a level of animosity far beyond anything seen during the Umbrella Movement. Protesters set fire to rubbish bins and tore up more than 2000 brick pavers to throw at police – some of who threw them right back. Police also responded with batons and pepper spray, and one officer even fired two live rounds from his service revolver as warning shots – something deeply shocking in Hong Kong, where gun violence is unheard of. Police estimated around 700 civilians were involved in the rioting, which lasted for ten hours before order was restored. More than eighty police officers and scores of protesters were injured, with around fifty people arrested.

While many in the community deplored the violence and the two largest pan-democrat parties, the Democratic Party and the Civic Party, quickly condemned the attacks on police, many of those involved were unrepentant. 'If history decides we're culpable for the violence, so be it,' said Edward Leung, one of the leaders of localist group Hong Kong Indigenous.[8] All of Hong Kong's university student unions issued statements in support of the protesters. A comment from an online commentator summed up the mood: 'Oppressive and outdated government policies and structural violence have created a situation where selling fishballs, a unique Hong Kong snack, on the street is outlawed, and selling and buying them is seen as a form of civil disobedience.'[9]

Subsequent events suggested that many Hong Kongers sympathised with the rioters, or at least with Hong Kong Indigenous and their political cause. Only a few weeks after the riots, Leung ran as a candidate in a LegCo by-election, and while he did not win the seat, he garnered 66 500 votes, representing 15 per cent of all the votes cast.[10]

Although righting the imbalance in favour of more democracy is one solution to Hong Kong's unique quandary, there is also another way to address the disequilibrium: reduce the rights and freedoms that Hong Kong enjoys. The post-Umbrella Movement period has seen pressure from Mainland and pro-Beijing elements in Hong Kong to do just that.

There have been indications that the Mainland authorities are increasing their activities in Hong

Kong under the auspices of the United Front Work Department, or UFWD. The UFWD is an agency under the Chinese Communist Party whose main function is to manage relations with non-Communist Party elites (people and groups holding social, commercial or academic influence), both inside and outside China, and to ensure that they are supportive of and useful to Communist Party rule.

Beijing authorities first began building their UFWD presence in Hong Kong in 1985 when the Xinhua News Agency opened representative offices in Hong Kong. After 1997, the official liaison role was taken over by the Central Government Liaison Office, and Beijing's community network and influence has increasingly been channelled through pro-Beijing political parties, in particular the Democratic Alliance for the Betterment and Progress of Hong Kong and the Federation of Trade Unions. With the financial backing and organisational support of the Mainland, these parties have rapidly expanded their grassroots network, providing various welfare services and gifts such as rice and cooking oil to elderly residents in public housing estates, as well as seasonal gifts like Mid-Autumn Festival moon cakes. In return for their support, Beijing loyalists are rewarded with various honours including appointments to national and local political bodies such as the National People's Congress, the Chinese People's Political Consultative

Conference and Hong Kong government advisory committees, as well as the nebulous promise of favourable 'business connections' in the Mainland.[11]

Recent reports suggest that, in response to the anti-government protests in Hong Kong, the UFWD (coordinating through the Central Government Liaison Office) has stepped up its activities in Hong Kong, not only to support the government but also to counter anti-government parties.[12] These activities frequently take the form of coordinating pro-government 'counter-protests', often with conspicuously well-organised and uniformly attired participants who possess unusually poor Cantonese skills, raising suspicions they have been bussed in from the Mainland.

Meanwhile, seemingly not sufficiently reassured by the existing structural bias favouring the pro-Beijing parties in the LegCo electoral system, and prompted by the rising localist movement represented by parties such as Hong Kong Indigenous, the Electoral Affairs Commission, or EAC, resorted to undertaking political screening of candidates for the LegCo elections held in September 2016.[13] All candidates were asked to sign an additional confirmation form declaring their adherence to certain selected provisions of the Basic Law which state that Hong Kong is an alienable part of China.[14] The process, of questionable legality to begin with, quickly devolved into farce when a number of traditional pan-democrat legislators refused to sign the declaration, but were nevertheless permitted to run, while Edward Leung of Hong Kong Indigenous signed the declaration but was still banned from running by the EAC because officials did not believe the sincerity of his declaration.[15]

The government strategy appeared to backfire, however, with localist candidates attracting broad community support in the subsequent election: candidates from localist-affiliated groups attracted a total of over 409 000 votes, representing 19 per cent of all votes cast in the election. Leung's nominated successor in the election, Sixtus 'Baggio' Leung, won a seat in the legislature,[16] as did another localist candidate, Lau Siu-lai – her activist track-record included facing charges for hawking fishballs without a licence on the night prior to the notorious Fishball Riot.[17] Notwithstanding these successes, with the EAC's political screening raising real questions about the fairness and legitimacy of the electoral process, the future of LegCo appears to be dim, giving even more impetus to popular movements.

Various actions by the PRC and Hong Kong governments have also tried to blur the distinction between the Mainland and Hong Kong. In a speech in September 2015, Zhang Xiaoming, head of the Central Government Liaison Office and Beijing's top official in Hong Kong, made a controversial speech entitled 'The correct understanding of Hong Kong's political system', in which he stated that Hong Kong does not implement the political system of separation of powers, and that the chief executive enjoys 'a special legal position which overrides administrative, legislative and judicial organs'.[18] The suggestion that the chief executive was above the law and the implied threat to judicial independence led to an outcry from the city's legal professionals and prompted a rare public rebuke from Chief Justice Geoffrey Ma, in which Ma highlighted relevant provisions of the Basic Law addressing judicial independence and equality before the law.[19] 'Everybody is equal before the law without exceptions,' he said. 'This applies to everyone.'[20]

The freedoms of expression and speech guaranteed under the Basic Law have traditionally safeguarded Hong Kong's lively media and publishing industry. However, this industry has increasingly come under attack. The largest book publisher and bookstore chain in the city, Sino United Publishing (which owns publishers and bookstore chains Joint Publishing, Chung Hwa Books and Commercial Press, operating fifty-one bookstores across the city), is indirectly owned by the Central Government Liaison Office. In this way, Beijing controls more than 80 percent of the publishing industry in Hong Kong.[21] Beijing's portfolio of Hong Kong media companies also includes three of Hong Kong's largest Chinese-language daily newspapers, *Wen*

Wei Po, *Ta Kung Pao* and *Hong Kong Commercial Daily*.

The abductions and arrests by Mainland authorities in 2015 and 2016 of a number of people associated with the Mighty Current Media publishing house and Causeway Bay Bookstore, which specialised in anti-Beijing titles for primarily Mainland audiences, sent a clear message: Hong Kong was not to be used as a base for publishing and distributing what Beijing regarded as subversive materials.[22]

Furthermore, the largely student-led Umbrella Movement protests demonstrated to Beijing that Hong Kong's university campuses are a potential source of subversion, making them an obvious target for a tightening of the screws, just as China's campuses were post-1989. University appointments will likely be subject to closer scrutiny in the future, with 'loyal' academics likely to receive honours and posts while their 'disloyal' colleagues are denied access to the Mainland to conduct research.[23]

The University of Hong Kong seems to have been singled out in particular – not least because Benny Tai is a member of its law faculty. In his 2015 policy address, Chief Executive C.Y. Leung specifically criticised the university's student magazine, *Undergrad*, for promoting Hong Kong self-determination.[24]

After former law dean Johannes Chan (seen by many as a pro-democracy sympathiser due to his defence of Tai on academic freedom grounds) was recommended by a nomination committee for a pro-vice chancellor position, pro-Beijing newspapers published critical commentaries attacking Chan. After months of delays, his appointment was rejected on spurious grounds by the Hong Kong University Council, which is stacked with pro-establishment figures directly appointed by the chief executive.[25]

Shortly after, C.Y. Leung rubbed salt into the wounds of the staff and students of the university by appointing controversial former education minister and pro-Beijing politician Arthur Li (nicknamed 'King Arthur' for his imperious style) as president of the university council. These incidents at the University of Hong Kong have only served to fuel concerns that academic freedom is under threat in Hong Kong.

The rule of law is another much-vaunted Core Value to be challenged in the post-Umbrella Movement era. During the Umbrella Movement protests, police repeatedly blamed protesters for undermining the rule of law through their 'prolonged unlawful assembly and blockage of roads', however, the rule of law is not actually undermined by people breaking the law. It happens every day – that's what a properly functioning justice system is intended to deal with.

Rather, the rule of law is undermined when the law is used as a tool to achieve a political end, as occurred when the Hong Kong government relied upon civil law injunctions as political cover to justify clearing the Umbrella Movement protest sites. In so doing, the government called the court system into service as a political tool. This politicisation of the courts has been called 'rule *by* law' – the use of the legal system by the government to rule its populace – a phrase frequently applied to the Mainland, but which could now be used with some justification to describe Hong Kong.[26]

Rule of law is also threatened when laws are either not enforced or enforced selectively. As an example, the government's prolonged inaction during the Umbrella Movement left significant space for triad gang activity. Allegations of selective policing and official acquiescence to triad gang involvement in various 'patriotic' support groups were never addressed or investigated by the government. What's more, police accused of carrying out assaults during the Umbrella Movement were never charged, while numerous protesters were charged on dubious grounds. Many people perceived this as a clear instance of criminal charges being used to intimidate or silence government critics.

Authorities have also turned their attention to online political activities. Police have been using the criminal charge of 'access to a computer with criminal or dishonest intent', an offence originally intended to be used against computer hackers and those guilty of online fraud, to suppress political speech online.[27] Since

June 2014, at least nine people have been arrested and charged under this provision simply for making online comments.[28] Continued use of this law presents a clear and present threat to freedom of speech in Hong Kong.

Finally, in the 2016 LegCo election, Beijing and its agents in Hong Kong engaged in a massive and coordinated voter-turnout effort – complete with the expected appeals to 'prosperity and stability' – in an attempt to break the pan-democrat parties' veto position in LegCo and prevent localist candidates winning any seats. Their efforts were an abject failure: pan-democrats and like-minded independents actually increased their total share of seats in LegCo, and one-fifth of Hong Kong's voters cast their votes in favour of radical anti-Beijing localist candidates. This would appear to be a stinging rejection of Beijing's recent policies towards Hong Kong. The question now will be whether this will lead to a rethink in Beijing and a more accommodating approach, or whether Beijing will double-down on its efforts to increase control and bring an unruly Hong Kong in to heel.

*

The Umbrella Movement blossomed out of Hong Kong people's desire for universal suffrage, which had been promised to them in the Sino-British Joint Declaration. The other key promise made in the Joint Declaration was that the Hong Kong way of life, with its attendant rights and freedoms, would remain 'unchanged for 50 years'. As 2047 approaches, finding a way to accommodate and balance these competing pressures will be an increasingly urgent priority for Hong Kong. The success of 'One Country, Two Systems' – and the preservation of Hong Kong's unique status in China and the world – depends upon getting this fragile balance right.

As long as the disequilibrium between rights and freedoms and representative democracy prevails in Hong Kong, the competing pressures to right that imbalance will also persist. And without more representative democracy, protest will continue to be a foundational form of political expression in Hong Kong.

The Umbrella Movement and all the protest movements that came before it were never just about the immediate issue at hand – whether universal suffrage or the protection of heritage buildings or support for democracy in Mainland China. These protests have always had at their core anxiety about Hong Kong's identity. Hong Kongers were told that the 1997 handover had finally determined the issue, righting the historical injustice of the Opium Wars and the Unequal Treaties that had ceded Hong Kong to the British. But in a world where self-determination has come to be seen as a fundamental right, Hong Kongers were told to forego that right, to content themselves with substituting one distant ruler for another. Through their protests, Hong Kong citizens seem to be asking again and again: What is Hong Kong's place in this post-colonial world?

Perhaps the protests will continue until Hong Kongers can answer this question for themselves.

NOTES

All websites last accessed November 2016.

Preface
1   Hong Kong Police Force, Public Order Event Statistics, available
     at: http://www.police.gov.hk/ppp_en/09_statistics/poes.html.
2   Centre of Social and Political Development Studies, Chinese
     University of Hong Kong, 'Press Conference on "Public Attitudes
     towards the Harmonious Society in Hong Kong"', 6 March 2012
     (Author's translation), available at: http://www.cuhk.edu.hk/hkiaps/
     csp/download/Press_Release_20120306.pdf.
3   Lonely Planet, 'Lonely Planet's Best in Travel: top 10 cities for
     2012', available at: https://www.lonelyplanet.com/england/london/
     travel-tips-and-articles/76861#.

I
1   The authoritative account of this period of Hong Kong's history,
     and the source for much of the information in this chapter, is Gary
     Ka-Wai Cheng, *Hong Kong's Watershed: The 1967 Riots*, Hong
     Kong University Press, Hong Kong, 2009. Further valuable mate-
     rial is contained in Christine Loh, *Underground Front: The Chinese
     Communist Party in Hong Kong*, Hong Kong University Press,
     Hong Kong, 2010.
2   Walsh, Frank, *A History of Hong Kong*, Harper Collins, London,
     1997, pp. 467–8.
3   Walsh, pp. 469–70. While the governor and Government House
     itself emerged from the protests unscathed, the same could not
     be said of the British Embassy in Beijing, which was burned

to the ground by Red Guards, and the fleeing staff beaten. See Percy Craddock, *Experiences of China*, John Murray, London, 1994.

4   Cheng, *Hong Kong's Watershed: The 1967 Riots*, p. 123.

5   For a broad discussion of the impact of the 1966 and 1967 riots and subsequent reforms, see Alan Smart and Tai-lok Lui, 'Learning from civil unrest: state/society relations in Hong Kong before and after the 1967 disturbances' in Robert Bickers and Ray Yep (eds.), *May Days in Hong Kong: Riot and Emergency in 1967*, Hong Kong University Press, Hong Kong, 2009.

6   Hong Kong Legislative Council, Official Report of Proceedings, Meeting of 15th November 1967, p. 476, available at: http://www.legco.gov.hk/1967/h671115.pdf.

7   Quoted in Cheng, *Hong Kong's Watershed: The 1967 Riots*, p. 140.

8   Cheng, *Hong Kong's Watershed: The 1967 Riots*, p. 128.

9   Editorial in the *People's Daily*, 8 March 1963, quoted in Cheng, *Hong Kong's Watershed: The 1967 Riots*, p. 128.

II

1   Wilson served as governor from April 1987 to July 1992, and was succeeded by Hong Kong's last governor, Christopher Patten. This anecdote was related to the author by a member of the British delegation. The horse-trading between the Chinese and British sides on the issue of elections was confirmed by David Wilson himself in an interview with the *South China Morning Post*: Gary Cheung, 'Beijing gave in to London on elected LegCo "at last minute"', *South China Morning Post*, 31 December 2014, available at: http://www.scmp.com/news/hong-kong/article/1671597/beijing-gave-london-elected-legco-last-minute.

2   Sino-British Joint Declaration, Article 3(4): 'The chief executive will be appointed by the Central People's Government on the basis of the results of elections or consultations to be held locally.'

3   Basic Law Article 45: 'The method for selecting the Chief Executive shall be specified in the light of the actual situation in the Hong Kong Special Administrative Region and in accordance with the principle of gradual and orderly progress. The ultimate aim is the selection of the Chief Executive by universal suffrage upon nomination by a broadly representative nominating committee in accordance with democratic procedures.'

4   Recounted in an interview with the Australian Broadcasting Corporation's *Four Corners* program, 'Secrets & Lies', broadcast 23 June 1997. Transcript available at: http://www.abc.net.au/4corners/stories/s72753.htm.

5   Ho, Andy, Chris Yeung and John Tang, 'Huge HK rally back students', *South China Morning Post*, 22 May 1989.

6   Yeung, Chris, 'Another vast crowd joins world-wide show of solidarity', *South China Morning Post*, 29 May 1989.

7   Both Martin Lee (founding chairman of the Democratic Party) and Emily Lau (chairman of the Democratic Party from 2012 through the time of publication) used the phrase: Australian Broadcasting Corporation, 'Secrets & Lies'.

8   Hong Kong Bill of Rights Ordinance, Chapter 383 of the Laws of Hong Kong, Articles 16, 17 and 18. See also: Yash P. Ghai, *The Hong Kong Bill of Rights: a comparative approach*, Butterworths Asia, Hong Kong, 1993.

9   Patten, Chris, 'Change-over will come and go, Hong Kong's here to stay', *South China Morning Post*, 1 July 1995.

10   Sino-British Joint Declaration, Article 3(5).

11   Decision of the National People's Congress Standing Committee on Treatment of Laws Previously in Force in Hong Kong in Accordance with Article 160 of the Basic Law of the HKSAR, Instrument 16, *Basic Law*, available at: http://www.basiclaw.gov.hk/en/basiclawtext/images/basiclawtext_doc16.pdf.

12   Public Order Ordinance (Chapter 245 of the Laws of Hong Kong), section 14. In addition to notifying the Commissioner of Police, a 'notice of no objection' must be received before a procession or gathering may proceed.

13   Public Order Ordinance (Chapter 245 of the Laws of Hong Kong), sections 7, 8, 9 and 17A.

14   Hong Kong SAR Chief Executive Policy Address 2015, paragraph 213, available at: http://www.policyaddress.gov.hk/2015/eng/index.html.

15   Cheung, Anthony B.L., 'The Hong Kong System under One Country Being Tested: Article 23, Governance Crisis and the Search for a New Hong Kong Identity' in Cheng, Joseph Y.S. (ed.), *The July 1 Protest Rally: Interpreting a Historic Event*, City University of Hong Kong Press, Hong Kong, 2005, p 65.

16   Leung, Ambrose and Gary Cheung, 'June 4 is history, I speak for HK, says Tsang – then has to apologise', *South China Morning Post*, 15 May 2009. See also: Eva Wu, 'Democrats call on Tsang to join July 1 rally', *South China Morning Post*, 7 June 2009.

III

1   Cheng, Joseph Y.S., 'Introduction: Causes and Implications of the July 1 Protest Rally in Hong Kong' in Cheng (ed.), *The July 1 Protest Rally: Interpreting a Historic Event*.

2   Cheng, *Hong Kong's Watershed: The 1967 Riots*, p. 6.

3   'Public order events' are public processions and meetings that
      require registration with the police. The last ten years' statistics are
      available at Hong Kong Police Force, Public Order Events Statis-
      tics: http://www.police.gov.hk/ppp_en/09_statistics/poes.html.

4   Cheung, Alvin Y.H., 'Hong Kong's Protests Are Not About the
      Economy, Stupid', *The Diplomat*, 3 October 2014. Available at:
      http://thediplomat.com/2014/10/hong-kongs-protests-are-not-
      about-the-economy-stupid/.

5   Each of the following sectors provides 300 representatives on the
      election committee: (i) Industrial, commercial and financial sectors;
      (ii) Professions; (iii) Labour, social services, religious and other sec-
      tors; and (iv) Legislative Council and other political bodies.

6   Voter Registration Statistics: Geographical Constituency, available
      at: http://www.voterregistration.gov.hk/eng/statistic20161.html.

7   Voter Registration Statistics: Functional Constituency, available at:
      http://www.voterregistration.gov.hk/eng/statistic20162.html.

8   'Pan-Democrat' parties include the Democratic Party, Civic Party,
      Labour Party, People Power, League of Social Democrats, Civic
      Passion and other parties and independent candidates generally
      regarded as sympathetic to those parties. For the first time in the
      2016 election, this group also included post-Umbrella Movement
      youth-led and 'localist' parties such as Demosistō and Youngspira-
      tion. 'Pro-Beijing' parties include the Democratic Alliance for the
      Betterment and Progress of Hong Kong, Liberal Party, Hong Kong
      Federation of Trade Unions, New People's Party and others. Refer-
      ences to 'parties' are for convenience only – party politics are lim-
      ited in Hong Kong. Under the current system, no party is able to
      become the 'ruling party', as the electoral system makes it difficult
      for any single party to win an absolute majority of the legislature.
      In any event, the chief executive, who wields all executive power,
      is forbidden from being a member of any political party. Moreover,
      there are no laws governing political parties in Hong Kong, so the
      existing political parties have no official status.

9   Pan-Democrats won nineteen out of the thirty-five geographic
      constituency seats as well as three out of five district council seats.

10   Pro-Beijing candidates won twenty-four out of thirty functional
      constituency seats.

11   Election results available at: http://www.elections.gov.hk/leg-
      co2016/eng/results.html. Analysis from *South China Morning Post*,
      '2016 Legislative Council election: Counting Room', available at:
      http://multimedia.scmp.com/counting-room/.

12   Cheung, Chor-yung, 'Hong Kong's Systemic Crisis of Govern-

ance and the Revolt of the "Post-80s" Youths' in Cheng (ed.), *New Trends of Political Participation in Hong Kong*, City University of Hong Kong Press, Hong Kong, 2014, pp. 420–4.

13 Hong Kong Basic Law, Article 74.

14 Hong Kong Basic Law, Annex II: Method for the Formation of the Legislative Council of the Hong Kong Special Administrative Region and Its Voting Procedure.

15 Cheung, Peter T.Y., 'Civic Engagement in the Policy Process in Hong Kong: Change and Continuity', *Public Administration and Development*, Vol. 31, 2001, pp. 113–21, at p. 114.

16 Hong Kong Basic Law, Article 23.

17 *Apple Daily*, 1 July 2003. The original Chinese reads: '走上街頭 不見不散'.

18 The University of Hong Kong Public Opinion Programme ('HKU-POP') survey reported an average of 462 000 participants and a peak of 502 000: https://www.hkupop.hku.hk/english/features/july1/headcount/2015/index.html.

19 Leung, Ambrose and Klaudia Lee, 'Hopes for freedom float upon a sea of political discontent', *South China Morning Post*, 2 July 2003, available at: http://www.scmp.com/article/420409/hopes-freedom-float-upon-sea-political-discontent.

20 *Ming Pao*, 23 September 2002, quoted in: Chan, Elaine and Joseph Chan, 'The First Ten Years of the HKSAR: Civil Society Comes of Age', *The Asia Pacific Journal of Public Administration*, Vol. 29, No. 1 (June 2007), 77-99, p. 82.

21 Organisers claimed a turnout of over 500 000; however, HKUPOP reported a peak of only 207000 demonstrators.

22 The increased number of Mainland visitors to Hong Kong resulting from this policy would later become the spark for protests after localist activists argued that Hong Kong was being overrun by Mainland visitors.

23 Cheung, 'Civic Engagement in the Policy Process in Hong Kong: Change and Continuity', p. 116.

24 Birdy Chu, *I Walk Therefore I am: A Record of Hong Kong Demonstrations*, Kubrick, Hong Kong, 2013, p. 235.

25 Many examples of Hong Kong protest props and artifacts could be seen in an exhibition curated by the Hong Kong Community Museum Project in 2004, catalogue available at: http://www.hkcmp.org/cmp/img/002_object/od_exbook.pdf.

IV

1 A comprehensive study of this topic is contained in Ng, Kai Hon, 'Social movements and policy capacity in Hong Kong: An

alternative perspective', *Issues & Studies*, Vol. 49, No. 2 (June 2013), pp. 179-214.

2   Chan and Chan, 'The First Ten Years of the HKSAR: Civil Society Comes of Age', p. 90.

3   Cheung, Anthony, 'The Rise of Identity Politics', *South China Morning Post*, 28 December 2006, available at: http://www.scmp.com/article/576763/rise-identity-politics.

4   Cheng, Joseph Yu-shek, 'The Emergence of Radical Politics in Hong Kong: Causes and Impact', *The China Review*, Vol. 14, No. 1 (Spring 2014), 199-232, p. 215.

5   Chan and Chan, 'The First Ten Years of the HKSAR: Civil Society Comes of Age', p. 90.

6   Quoted in Vaudine England, 'Protesters fight to save historic Hong Kong pier', *The Guardian*, 18 June 2007, available at: http://www.theguardian.com/world/2007/jun/18/china.international.

7   Cartier, Carolyn, 'Culture and the City: Hong Kong, 1997-2007', *China Review*, Vol. 8, No. 1 (Spring 2008), pp. 59–83, p. 77.

8   Hong Kong Government press release, 民政事務局局長就文物建築保護政策諮詢的發言要點 (Highlights of Speech by Secretary for Home Affairs Bureau on Consultation on Heritage Building Protection Policy), 8 January 2007 (Author's translation), available at: http://www.info.gov.hk/gia/general/200701/08/P200701080243.htm.

9   Hong Kong Government, Civil Engineering and Development Department, 'Reassembly of Queen's Pier', available at: http://www.queenspier.hk.

10   'Choice memories', *South China Morning Post*, 24 July 2004, available at: http://www.scmp.com/article/464048/choice-memories.

11   Urban Renewal Authority, 'URA announces $3.58 billion project in Wan Chai', 17 October 2003, available at: http://www.ura.org.hk/en/media/press-release/2003/20031017.aspx.

12   Lee, Eliza Wing-yee, 'Civil society organizations and local governance in Hong Kong', in Stephen Wing-kai Chiu and Siu-lun Wong (eds.), *Repositioning the Hong Kong Government: Social Foundations and Political Challenges*, Hong Kong University Press, Hong Kong, 2012, pp. 147–64, at p. 156.

13   Lai, Chloe, 'No promotion is needed for our shops… business comes naturally' *South China Morning Post*, 9 February 2004, available at: http://www.scmp.com/article/443815/no-promotion-needed-for-our-shopsbusiness-comes-naturally.

14   Urban Renewal Authority, 'Local Characters reinforced by a Thematic Wedding City in Wan Chai', 20 December 2007, available at: http://www.ura.org.hk/en/media/press-re-

lease/2007/20071220.aspx.

15   Ng, 'Social movements and policy capacity in Hong Kong: An alternative perspective', p. 205.

16   A comprehensive overview of this protest campaign is available in: Cheung, 'Hong Kong's Systemic Crisis of Governance and the Revolt of the "Post 80s" Youths – The Anti-Express Rail Campaign'.

17   Fung, Owen and Christy Leung, 'Uproar at LegCo after snap vote leads to passage of HK$19.6 billion for Hong Kong high-speed rail link', *South China Morning Post*, 11 March 2016, available at: http://www.scmp.com/news/hong-kong/economy/article/1923130/uproar-legco-after-snap-vote-leads-passage-hk196-billion-hong.

18   See Partnerships for Community Development, '"Going Local" Campaign Led to a Revolution to Preserve Farmland – Experience of the "Pak Heung People Eat Pak Heung Vegetables" Project', available at: http://www.pcd.org.hk/en/work/going-local-campaign-led-revolution-preserve-farmland—experience-"pak-heung-people-eat-pak.

19   Cheung, Tony, 'A history of how national education was introduced in Hong Kong', *South China Morning Post*, 9 September 2012, available at: http://www.scmp.com/news/hong-kong/article/1032512/history-how-national-education-was-introduced-hong-kong.

20   中國模式：國情專題教學手冊 (The China Model: National Education Handbook), National Education Services Centre, Hong Kong, 2012. Author's translation.

21   Lau, Joyce, 'Thousands Protest China's Plans for Hong Kong Schools', *New York Times*, 29 July 2012, available at: http://www.nytimes.com/2012/07/30/world/asia/thousands-protest-chinas-curriculum-plans-for-hong-kong-schools.html.

22   Lai, Alexis, '"National education" raises furor in Hong Kong', CNN, 30 July 2012, available at: http://edition.cnn.com/2012/07/30/world/asia/hong-kong-national-education-controversy/.

23   'State brainwashing perfectly all right, liaison official blogs', *South China Morning Post*, 12 May 2011, available at: http://www.scmp.com/article/967464/state-brainwashing-perfectly-all-right-liaison-official-blogs.

24   Hong Kong Government, 'Press statement by Committee on the Initiation of Moral and National Education Subject', 8 October 2012, available at: http://www.info.gov.hk/gia/general/201210/08/P201210080555.htm.

V
1   Basic Law Article 45.

2   The full text of the white paper 'The Practice of the "One Country, Two Systems" Policy in the Hong Kong Special Administrative Region' is available on the website of the Commissioner's Office of China's Foreign Ministry in Hong Kong at: http://www.fmcoprc.gov.hk/eng/xwdt/gsxw/t1164057.htm.

3   Ibid.

4   See: 'White Paper on the Practice of "One Country, Two Systems" Policy in the Hong Kong Special Administrative Region: Response of the Hong Kong Bar Association', 11 June 2014, para 7: 'Judges and judicial officers of the HKSAR are not to be regarded as part of "Hong Kong's administrators" or part of the governance team upon whom a political requirement is imposed.' Available at: http://www.hkba.org/sites/default/files/White_Paper_Response_eng.pdf.

5   The Law Society of Hong Kong, press release, 19 August 2014, available at: http://www.hklawsoc.org.hk/pub_e/news/press/20140819.asp.

6   HKUPOP reported a peak of 166 000 while protest organisers claimed 510 000 had taken part: https://www.hkupop.hku.hk/english/features/july1/headcount/2015/index.html.

7   Tai, Yiu-ting Benny, 公民抗命的最大殺傷力武器 (The most powerful weapon in civil disobedience), *Hong Kong Economic Journal*, 16 January 2013, available at: http://oclp.hk/index.php?route=occupy/article_detail&article_id=23.

8   In Chinese: 讓愛與和平佔領中環.The movement was officially launched on 27 March 2013. See Joshua But, 'Occupy Central Hong Kong supporters ready to block traffic and go to jail for democracy', *South China Morning Post*, 28 March 2013, available at: http://www.scmp.com/news/hong-kong/article/1201371/occupy-central-supporters-ready-block-traffic-and-go-jail-democracy.

9   Full text of the decision is available at: http://news.xinhuanet.com/english/china/2014-08/31/c_133609238.htm.

10   Joshua Wong speech in Umbrella Square, heard by the author, October 2014.

11   An English language transcript of the televised footage of the 18 May 1989 meeting between Li Peng and the Chinese student leaders is available at: http://www.tsquare.tv/chronology/May18mtg.html.

12   Opening remarks by Assistant Commissioner of Police at press conference, 9 December 2014, available at: http://www.info.gov.hk/gia/general/201412/09/P201412091047.htm.

13   Interview with the author, December 2014.

14   Interview with the author, December 2014.

15   Interview with the author, December 2014.

16 Public Opinion Program, University of Hong Kong, 'Rating of
    Top Ten Political Groups', pp. 20–3, October 2014, available at:
    https://www.hkupop.hku.hk/english/popexpress/pgrating/datata-
    bles/datatable67.html.

17 Lam, Jeffie and Joyce Ng, 'Is this goodbye to Occupy Central?
    Co-founder Benny Tai admits, "We failed"', *South China Morning
    Post*, 2 September 2014, available at: http://www.scmp.com/news/
    hong-kong/article/1583636/occupy-centrals-strategy-has-failed-
    and-support-waning-benny-tai.

18 Ng, Joyce, 'Hong Kong's Occupy protests did not end with a loss,
    says co-founder Benny Tai', *South China Morning Post*, 22 De-
    cember 2014, available at: http://www.scmp.com/news/hong-kong/
    article/1667605/hong-kongs-occupy-protests-did-not-end-loss-
    says-co-founder-benny-tai.

19 Interview with the author, December 2014.

20 Sala, Ilaria Maria, 'Eddie Chu Hoi-dick, environmentalist and ani-
    mal rights activist, is the surprise winner in Hong Kong's election',
    Quartz, 5 September 2016, available at: http://qz.com/773932/
    eddie-chu-hoi-dick-environmentalist-and-animal-rights-activist-is-
    the-surprise-winner-in-hong-kongs-election/.

21 LegCo election turnout figures available at: http://www.elections.
    gov.hk/legco2016/eng/turnout.html.

VI

1   See: Patten, Chris, 'The city will not sleep', *The Guardian*, 30
    June 2007, available at: http://www.theguardian.com/commentis-
    free/2007/jun/30/comment.china. See also Hui, Victoria Tin-bor,
    'The Protests and Beyond', *Journal of Democracy*, Vol. 26, No. 2,
    April 2015, pp. 111–21, p. 118.

2   Hui, 'The Protests and Beyond', p. 119.

3   The phrase was first used by Benny Tai prior to the start of the
    Umbrella Movement: Buckley, Chris and Michael Forsythe,
    'China Restricts Voting Reforms for Hong Kong', *New York Times*,
    31 August 2014, available at: http://www.nytimes.com/2014/09/01/
    world/asia/hong-kong-elections.html. For predictions post-Umbrel-
    la Movement see Fion Li and Dominic Lau, 'Occupy Hong Kong
    End Marks Start of "Permanent" Political Unrest', *Bloomberg*, 12
    December 2014, available at: http://www.bloomberg.com/news/
    articles/2014-12-11/occupy-hong-kong-end-marks-start-of-perma-
    nent-political-unrest.

4   'Five arrested in Mong Kok scuffle', *China Daily Asia*, 29
    June 2015, available at: http://www.chinadailyasia.com/
    hknews/2015-06/29/content_15283116.html.

5   Yuen, Chantal, 'Protesters rally against Pikachu's new name at Japanese consulate', *Hong Kong Free Press*, 30 May 2016, available at: https://www.hongkongfp.com/2016/05/30/protesters-rally-against-pikachus-new-name-at-japanese-consulate/.

6   Wong, Vicky, 'Protesters march to High Court over 'breast assault' conviction', *Hong Kong Free Press*, 27 July 2015, available at: https://www.hongkongfp.com/2015/07/27/protesters-march-to-high-court-over-breast-assault-conviction/.

7   A detailed timeline of the events are available in *Hong Kong Economic Journal*, '12 hours of Mong Kok clashes: A timeline', 11 February 2016, available at: http://www.ejinsight.com/20160211-twelve-hours-of-mong-kok-clashes/.

8   Wong, Alan, 'China Labels Protesters "Radical Separatists," and They Agree', *New York Times*, 20 February 2016, available at: http://www.nytimes.com/2016/02/21/world/asia/hong-kong-indige-nous-separatism.html.

9   Leung, Michael, comment on Instagram photos of the Fishball Riots, available at: https://instagram.com/p/BBi-ZQxqXHP/.

10   Cheung, Karen, '"A turning point": Pro-democracy Civic Party's Alvin Yeung wins NT East by-election with 37% of votes', *Hong Kong Free Press*, 29 February 2016, available at: https://www.hongkongfp.com/2016/02/29/a-turning-point-civic-partys-alvin-yeung-wins-new-territories-east-by-election-with-37-of-votes/.

11   Cheng, 'The Emergence of Radical Politics in Hong Kong: Causes and Impact', pp. 214–5.

12   Torode, Greg, James Pomfret and Benjamin Kang Lim, 'The battle for Hong Kong's soul', *Reuters*, 1 July 2014, available at: http://www.reuters.com/article/us-hongkong-china-specialreport-idUSK-BN0F62XU20140702.

13   Webb, David, 'A Sordid Electoral Affair', *Webb Site*, 17 August 2016, available at: https://webb-site.com/articles/legco2016.asp.

14   Electoral Affairs Commission, 'Press statement by EAC on 2016 Legislative Council Election', 14 July 2016, available at: http://www.info.gov.hk/gia/general/201607/14/P2016071400441.htm.

15   Cheng, Kris, 'Edward Leung has not genuinely switched from pro-independence stance, says election official', *Hong Kong Free Press*, 2 August 2016, available at: https://www.hongkongfp.com/2016/08/02/edward-leung-not-genuinely-switched-pro-inde-pendence-stance-says-election-official/.

16   Cheung, Gary and Jeffie Lam, 'Rise of localists in Hong Kong polls set to bring headaches for Beijing, analysts say', *South China Morning Post*, 5 September 2016, available at: http://www.scmp.com/news/hong-kong/politics/article/2015349/rise-localists-hong-

kong-polls-set-bring-headaches-beijing.

17   Lau, Chris, 'Hong Kong woman accused of hawking without a
      licence blames "unscrupulous government"', *South China Morning
      Post*, 1 March 2016, available at: http://www.scmp.com/news/
      hong-kong/law-crime/article/1919096/hong-kong-woman-accused-
      hawking-without-licence-blames.

18   Khan, Natasha, 'China Official Says Hong Kong Chief Above
      Judiciary, Legislature', *Bloomberg*, 13 September 2015, available
      at: http://www.bloomberg.com/news/articles/2015-09-13/china-of-
      ficial-says-hong-kong-chief-above-judiciary-legislature. The original
      Chinese transcript of the speech is available at: http://www.locpg.
      hk/jsdt/2015-09/12/c_128222889.htm.

19   'Statement of the Hong Kong Bar Association on the Speech of Di-
      rector Zhang Xiaoming at the Seminar held on 12 September 2015
      marking the 25th Anniversary of the Promulgation of the Basic
      Law of the Hong Kong Special Administrative Region', available
      at: http://hkba.org/sites/default/files/20150914%20-%20Press%20
      Statement%20of%20HKBA%20-%20English.pdf.

20   See: 'Transcript of remarks by Chief Justice', 16 September
      2015, available at: http://www.info.gov.hk/gia/general/201509/16/
      P201509160582.htm.

21   Mudie, Luisetta, 'Fears For Hong Kong's Independent Publishers
      After China Book Chain Takeover', *Radio Free Asia*, 9 April 2015,
      available at: http://www.rfa.org/english/news/china/china-book-
      chain-takeover-04092015121452.html. See also: Ilaria Maria Sala,
      'Creeping censorship in Hong Kong: how China controls sale of
      sensitive books', *The Guardian*, 19 May 2015, available at: http://
      www.theguardian.com/world/2015/may/19/censorship-in-hong-
      kong-how-china-controls-sale-of-sensitive-books.

22   Forsyth, Michael, 'Disappearance of 5 Tied to Publisher Prompts
      Broader Worries in Hong Kong', *New York Times*, 4 January
      2016, available at: http://www.nytimes.com/2016/01/05/world/
      asia/mighty-current-media-hong-kong-lee-bo.html. The Hong
      Kong airport subsequently announced that it would close down a
      number of bookshops and replace those operated by Singaporean
      chain Page One (popular with Mainland travellers buying books
      and magazines banned across the border) with stores operated
      by Sino United. See: Simon Parry, 'Hong Kong airport cuts back
      on bookshops: Page One out, new mainland-based operator takes
      over', *South China Morning Post*, 27 March 2016, available at:
      http://www.scmp.com/news/hong-kong/education-community/arti-
      cle/1931064/hong-kong-airport-cuts-back-bookshops-page-one.

23   Denyer, Simon, 'Is Hong Kong's academic freedom under Chinese

attack?', *The Washington Post*, 13 March 2015, available at: https://www.washingtonpost.com/world/asia_pacific/is-hong-kongs-academic-freedom-under-chinese-attack/2015/03/12/8680fc60-e819-4ed0-9097-04a9774cfd35_story.html.

24 Hong Kong SAR Chief Executive Policy Address 2015, para 10, available at: http://www.policyaddress.gov.hk/2015/eng/index.html.

25 Cheng, Kris, 'Explainer: The HKU Council pro-vice-chancellor debate', *Hong Kong Free Press*, 30 September 2015, available at: https://www.hongkongfp.com/2015/09/30/explainer-hku-council-rejects-johannes-chan-appointment-to-pro-vice-chancellor/.

26 For a discussion of the distinction between 'rule of law' and 'rule by law' in the Mainland China context, see Nesossi, Elisa, 'Interpreting the rule of law in China', *Made In China*, Issue 2, 2016, available at: http://www.chinoiresie.info/PDF/MADE-IN-CHINA-ISSUE2_06072016.pdf.

27 Crimes Ordinance (Chapter 200 of the Laws of Hong Kong), section 161.

28 Zhang, Jennifer, 'Hong Kong's Activist Social Media Culture Under Threat', *The Diplomat*, 14 June 2015, available at: http://thediplomat.com/2015/06/hong-kongs-activist-social-media-culture-under-threat/.

PHOTOGRAPHS

All photographs courtesy and copyright of the author.

ACKNOWLEDGEMENTS

Many thanks to Peter Cai, John Garnaut and Stuart Leavenworth for providing me with the opportunity to publish my writing on the Umbrella Movement.

I am grateful to Jeremy Goldkorn, Imogen Liu for her support of this project and invaluable editorial guidance, and Sam Chow Hok Lam and Angela Luk for research assistance.

My thanks also to the Asian Law Centre at the University of Melbourne and the Hong Kong Public Affairs and Social Service Society at the London School of Economics, whose invitations to speak on the Umbrella Movement prompted me to develop many of the ideas in this book.

I would like to thank my family for their support. This book is for Agnes, who lived it with me, and Marcus, a child of the revolution.

PENGUIN
SPECIALS

The Inaugural
Hong Kong Series

Hong Kong has many faces: international financial hub, home of martial arts movies and Canto-pop, intercultural melting pot, former Crown colony and today, Special Administrative Region of the People's Republic of China. When the United Kingdom transferred sovereignty over Hong Kong to China on 1 July 1997, the event not only ended 156 years of British rule, but it also opened a new chapter of cultural, linguistic and political exploration. Twenty years later, Penguin Random House launches the Hong Kong Specials series. Seven outstanding literary and intellectual voices from Hong Kong take stock of the city as it is today, a city that has undergone an era of unforeseeable transition and is now in the midst of reconstructing its own identity.

Read more from these authors in the series:

Xu Xi
Antony Dapiran
Dung Kai-cheung
Simon Cartledge
Ben Bland
Christopher DeWolf
Magnus Renfrew

PENGUIN
SPECIALS

Cantonese Love Stories
DUNG KAI-CHEUNG

Translated from the original Chinese by Bonnie S. McDougall and Anders Hansson

Twenty-five Vignettes of a City

A collection of twenty-five narrative sketches, *Cantonese Love Stories* offers an intimate look into the cultural, commercial and romantic milieu of Hong Kong in the 1990s. Two lovers ruminate on the power of their photo booth stickers to keep them together. Peach-pocket Girl reads stolen love letters at a café. Pui Pui knows a Portuguese egg tart is authentic if she dreams of riding a boat-like egg tart. Each character inhabits a different corner of Hong Kong's dreamscape; together they bring to life Dung Kai-cheung's imaginative vision of the city.

Dung Kai-Cheung is an award-winning fiction writer, playwright and essayist born and based in Hong Kong. He is the author of numerous works, including *Atlas: The Archeology of an Imaginary City* and *Histories of Time*.

'Dung's experimental prose and philosophic language games will appeal to readers of Italo Calvino, Jorge Louis Borges, and Paul Auster, and will find camaraderie here.'
Los Angeles Review of Books

'For the past two decades, Dung Kai-cheung's voice has been the single most innovative on the Hong Kong literary scene'
Michael Berry, author of *A History of Pain: Trauma in Modern Chinese Literature and Film*

'Well worth the experiment.'
Asian Review of Books